# saving safa

## waris dirie

### with Walter Lutschinger

### Translated by Ruth Martin

virago

VIRAGO

First published in Germany in 2013 by Knaur Verlag
First published in Great Britain in 2015 by Virago Press

1 3 5 7 9 10 8 6 4 2

A CIP catalogue record for this book
is available from the British Library.

ISBN 978-0-349-00596-6

Typeset in New Baskerville by M Rules
Printed and bound in Great Britain by
Clays Ltd, St Ives plc

Papers used by Virago are from well-managed forests
and other responsible sources.

MIX
Paper from
responsible sources
FSC
www.fsc.org    FSC® C104740

Virago Press
An imprint of
Little, Brown Book Group
Carmelite House
50 Victoria Embankment
London EC4Y 0DZ

An Hachette UK Company
www.hachette.co.uk

www.virago.co.uk

Waris Dirie is an internationally renowned model and was a face of Revlon skin-care products. In 1997 she was appointed by the United Nations as special ambassador for women's rights in Africa, in its effort to eliminate the practice of female genital mutilation. In 2007 Waris Dirie was made a Chevalier de la Légion d'Honneur by the French Government.

*Also by Waris Dirie*

Desert Flower

Desert Dawn

Desert Children

# Prologue

*Djibouti, 15 January 2013*

*Dear Waris Dirie*

*My name is Safa Nour and I am seven years old. I
acted in your film, do you remember? I come from Djibouti
and I have two brothers, Amir and Nour, and my Maman
and my Papa.*

*All the people in Balbala know me because of your film.
That makes me proud.*

*Papa says that we are doing much better now, we have
things to eat and even light. The others don't have that.
And I go to school, that is great! Everyone there knows
who you are as well, and that I acted in your film.*

*Papa always says we are also famous now.*

*How are you? I am well, but sometimes I am also very
sad because I am all alone. When we play on the street, the*

*children run away and curse and say bad things. They say
I stink, but that's not true at all. Maman and Papa also
argue because of me and Maman cries a lot, Safa is a
disgrace, she is not circumcised! And Papa gets very cross.*

    *If I was circumcised too, then the others would play with
me, but I am also scared because it hurts a lot. So I also
don't want it. I don't know, what do you say?*

**Safa, our little Desert Flower.**

*The children at school are much nicer, but not in the beginning. Do you know, the other children have important parents and they come from many faraway countries. I am the only one from Balbala and we are not rich, so they were mean and because of my niqab too.*

*Then Mme Dourani talked to Maman and now I always go to school without my niqab, and I like that better too.*

*My best friend is called Diane Pearl and she comes from America. Her father is a diplomat, I don't know what that means, what is that Waris? Diane lives in the most beautiful house in the whole of Djibouti and she is eight already. Diane is not very good at French, that's why she is in my class. We get on really well and everyone knows she is my friend, Diane is also tall and now the other children aren't mean any more.*

*A few days ago people came to see us with cameras and microphones and they talked to everyone and asked Maman and Papa lots of things. They also gave me a picture of you and I look at it when I am sad, that's why I am writing to you.*

*You are the most beautiful woman and the strongest. You are so great!*

*When I grow up I want to be just like you.*

*When will you come and visit me?*

*Are you coming back to Djibouti?*

*That would be lovely.*

*I love you,*

*Safa*
*With help from Fardouza*

Safa with her best friend Diane in school.

I reread the words of this little girl from Balbala, a suburb of Djibouti City. I had received plenty of moving letters from women – from victims who wrote to ask my Desert Flower Foundation for help; from wealthy and respected women offering me their support; and from frightened women begging me to free them from their misery. But I had never received a letter like this from such a young girl.

I sat in my hotel room in Brussels, going over and over Safa's words. They were like a snare around my heart. What kind of trouble must this little girl be suffering – at just seven years old – to make her seek help to write such an unusually long and grown-up letter? On the one hand happy to be unharmed, and on the other ignored, shunned and lonely . . .

'Safa wrote this letter with our team in Balbala for you. I had to make her a solemn promise that I would give it to you in person,' said my assistant and manager, Joanna, interrupting the emotional merry-go-round in my head.

I wanted to see the videos of her village and her family.

'Safa says you conducted interviews there? I'd like to see everything you've got.'

'No problem, I have everything here,' Joanna reassured me. 'As soon as we get back to the hotel I'll bring it all up to your room.'

I folded the letter carefully and put it into the inside pocket of my jacket, close to my heart, which it had just touched so deeply.

# I

# The message

My throat feels constricted and I gasp for air. My hands
start to tremble and perspire, fumbling the arms of the
grey leather chair. I need something to cling to. I want to
get out of here. I don't want to look. These images have
appeared in front of my eyes all too often before. I know
I won't be able to look away this time, either. I can feel the
blood pulsing in my temples, as if my head is about to
explode at any minute. I am terrified. The darkened hall
seems to be getting smaller and narrower by the second.
But I am trapped: trapped in yesterday.

Then there is a shrill cry. It echoes through the conference room – it goes right through me. A little girl's face,
distorted with pain, appears before my eyes. There is blood
everywhere. A twig is broken off a thorn bush; rough,
bony, furrowed hands snap the razor-sharp thorns from
the gnarled branch. The face of an old witch. Destructive,
dogged, ugly, with eyes so cold they send a shiver down my

spine. Two hands grasp the little girl's legs and wrench them apart.

Unflinching and determined, the hands belong to the child's mother.

She will destroy her tiny daughter's life for ever. How could she do something so cruel to her own child, her own flesh and blood? Why doesn't she snatch up her little girl and run away with her? After all, she has already lost one daughter, who bled to death as a result of the murderess's cutting and stitching. And now? Will this girl survive?

Later, when her grown-up daughter asks her why this was done to her, she will say it was the will of Allah. That the tradition of her people demanded it. That it was the only way for her to be a good, faithful, pure wife. That they would otherwise never have been able to find a husband who would pay a decent bride-price for her. That it was done for her own safety. That it had always been done in her tribe, and always would be. That being a woman entails suffering and submission.

I know all that.

A tremendous rage builds up inside me. Tears of anger and despair well up in my eyes and stream down my face. There is only one thought in my mind: This has to stop. This has to stop once and for all.

The lights went up in the auditorium of the Berlaymont building in Brussels. I hurriedly wiped the tears from my cheeks and looked around. I was at an international conference against female genital mutilation, having been invited by the Vice-President of the European Commission. The savage circumcision scene from the film *Desert*

*Flower* had opened the conference. EU commissioners, ministers, legislators, representatives of various non-profit organisations and journalists were looking at the screen beyond me with shocked expressions. They were all familiar with my 1998 book of the same name, where I wrote about the mutilation that was done to me as a five-year-old, and how I ran away from home. Many of those present had read it, and a few had also seen the film, which was released in cinemas in 2009. All the same, the horror was written large on each of their faces. In the audience sat several top politicians from Europe and Africa, as well as high-ranking EU officials and representatives of important non-governmental organisations. They all had it in their power to protect hundreds of thousands of girls from genital mutilation. To look after the victims. To make their lives worthwhile again.

It was a puzzle to me why they weren't doing it. Why they didn't just do the work they were being paid for.

They watched in silence as I made my way to the lectern, trying to collect myself, to push to the back of my mind the gruesome scene that had shaped me and my life.

'Here. Waris.' From her seat in the front row, Joanna passed me a tissue.

My assistant, manager and right-hand woman – and so much more. In the course of the years we had spent together fighting female genital mutilation, or FGM as it is known internationally, she had become my closest confidante and most faithful friend.

Joanna knew what the images in the circumcision scene did to me. I had seen *Desert Flower* dozens of times, at premières and presentations all over the world. I even had a hand in making the film, and had been in favour of shooting the mutilation in the most extreme way we could. Of course, it was impossible to depict the true horror and brutality of the procedure which around three million girls worldwide suffer every year, when their clitoris and their inner and outer labia are hacked away with a dirty razor blade while they are fully conscious, and the bloody remains of the labia sown together.

The screams of the little girl playing me on the cinema screen gave me a flashback to that pain every time I heard them. Countless times after viewing the scene, Joanna had hugged me and done her best to comfort me. This time, too, she was looking deep into my eyes from the front row, nodding to give me courage as she had so often done before.

A few hours before my presentation, I had met the Vice-President of the European Commission, who was also the commissioner for the Department of Justice, Fundamental Rights and Citizenship, in her office.

'Waris, I'm so glad you've come back to Brussels!' Viviane Reding greeted me with a warm smile.

Her blue eyes sparkled through elegant, rimless glasses. 'Together we'll bring this issue into the public eye: people need to hear all about it,' Reding went on determinedly, folding her arms.

For a moment I was speechless. And then I snorted: 'Bring it into the public eye?' When the Vice-President didn't react, I snapped.

'Since 1996, I've been doing nothing but informing people about FGM. I've given speeches to the UN in New York, to the European Union here in Brussels, to the African Union in Addis Ababa, and to governments all over the world. I've appeared on dozens of talk shows, given countless interviews, and bared my soul – sacrificing my own privacy in order to open people's eyes.' I had started to raise my voice, and now it began to waver. 'I've been a special envoy for the UN and the African Union, and I started the Desert Flower Foundation. For years I've put every last drop of energy into the fight against genital mutilation all over the world. And you're still trying to talk to me about how best to bring this issue into the public eye?'

When Reding was able to look me in the eye again, I went on more quietly, but with even more determination, 'I am not here to raise awareness. I am here to stamp out FGM, this crime against little girls, once and for all – with your help. There's been more than enough talk already. I want to see action now. From the European Union, and from all the governments in Europe.'

In 2006, soon after the publication of my third book, *Desert Children*, I had appeared before the EU Cabinet to present the worrying findings from my Desert Flower Foundation's research on the continuing spread of FGM in Europe. My team and I had even put together a catalogue of suggested measures, which I set out to Europe's decision-makers. And which of these concrete ideas and suggestions had even been partially implemented?

None of them.

Meanwhile, millions of girls and women continued to be cut – girls and women who either die a miserable death from an infection, or have to live with terrible pain.

'How are you going to protect young girls from being destroyed for ever? And how are you planning to help people who are already victims?' I pressed her.

Reding's office door swung open. She quickly pulled herself together, threw up her arms and embraced the visitor. 'Waris, my dear, may I introduce you to the First Lady of Burkina Faso, Chantal Compaoré? Her government has had more success in the fight against FGM than any other in Africa.'

There was a storm of camera flashes, and microphones everywhere. Three film crews and two photographers were bobbing and weaving frantically around the popular First Lady, who was swathed in colourful robes. That brought my conversation with the Vice-President to an end – but my fighting spirit had been reawakened.

Many years ago I realised that politicians from several countries were using me as a token. A single photo with Waris Dirie and an emotionally phrased caption would give credence to the action they were supposedly taking on FGM. I had been in demand as a 'star guest' at international conferences for years. Each time, I was allowed to present my demands, and then put on a nice smile as I posed for group pictures with presidents and ministers. There was just one thing I wasn't allowed to do: come back later and ask which of those demands had actually been put into action, or what specific steps they were taking to support my fight against FGM.

Recently I had started accepting only a very few invitations from politicians, preferring to concentrate on the work of the Desert Flower Foundation. I had spent a long time mulling over whether I should really take part in the European Commission's conference. But the hope that this time I might finally be able to negotiate rigorous sanctions had finally led me to Brussels.

*

As I reached the lectern, I placed my hand over my left jacket pocket, where I had put Safa's letter. How true to life her portrayal of me, the little Waris, had been in the film, when she was just three years old! And so far, she had been spared the cruel act of circumcision. At least, that was what she said in her letter. But was my little desert flower in danger of being cut, in spite of our agreement?

I tried to put my thoughts in order, and took several deep breaths

'Vice-President, commissioners and representatives,' I began. The eyes of around a hundred experts and interested listeners were on me. 'In January 2006, here in this building, I presented the Council of Ministers with the results of two years' research, financed by my Desert Flower Foundation without any kind of public funding. I brought not just my manifesto, but also a list of measures that all governments could take to fight FGM. And I showed how we can help the victims in a respectful manner. All the ministers and EU commissioners were impressed; they applauded; they promised me they would put these demands into action. And what has happened since then?'

I looked around. There was an awkward silence in the hall.

'Nothing.

'Now you have invited me here again, to discuss what measures the EU and the governments of Europe can take against FGM. It's as though everything we discussed in 2006 has been forgotten. And so I have brought my manifesto again, together with all my demands, which are also on my foundation's website. I would like to urge you once more to read them carefully, and implement these measures at long last!'

I held the papers above my head insistently, so that even the people in the back rows could see them.

'Ladies and gentlemen, all of you' – I pointed my finger at the rows in the hall – 'every single one of you has it in your power! Paediatricians, gynaecologists, midwives, teachers, asylum support workers, social workers, youth workers, police officers, public prosecutors and judges right across Europe must be informed and trained. This is the only way for all of us to work together and put a stop to this crime once and for all. The measures I have suggested are as simple as they are effective. Don't you *want* to protect these innocent girls? Do you really not want to help the victims?'

The silence in the room was oppressive and liberating at once. I had finally voiced the frustration that had been weighing on my heart for years. I seized the moment and carried on speaking.

'Why do you keep holding conferences if you don't do anything afterwards? The point of these events is not to help you get re-elected; it's to help little girls like the one you've just seen in the film. Safa's family is originally from Somalia, just like me. Her life seemed to be laid out for her. But then she got a part in my film, and her life changed. The film role protected Safa from the genital mutilation her parents were planning. She's seven years old now and goes to school regularly, which means she has a chance to choose what she does with her life. But one Safa is not enough: we need a million Safas – in Africa, Asia and Europe – and we can only save them with your help. Only with your help can we give these innocent girls a life worth living. I therefore implore you to *do* something.'

*

'Well done, Waris!'

In the corridor outside the conference room, Joanna hugged me tightly. I didn't say anything; I was too much in turmoil, drained and tired and stunned by it all.

'I shouldn't have shown that scene,' I sighed when we were in the taxi. 'It stirs everything up again too much, every time. And the moment is so true to life that for a second, even I believe the images are real.'

Joanna gave me a sympathetic look. We had often talked about how the film took me back to my child-hood. Back to the Somali desert, under an endless sky; that, to me, was the most beautiful place on earth. We had often gone hungry, and hardly ever had enough water to drink. But in spite of that I had been happy. I knew no fear, even though many dangers were lurking in the arid landscape. My parents had taught me to be alert and I knew my way around the desert. If I hadn't, I would never have been able to cross it alone at the age of just thirteen, to escape my father's plan to marry me to an old man. I loved my home – and my mother, whom I trusted blindly. At least until that horrific, blood-soaked day when I was five.

'Waris, showing that scene was the right thing to do,' Joanna replied. 'Remember why you insisted that the cir-cumcision scene mustn't be left out of the film? It was there to open people's eyes. Your instinct was right. Plus,' she went on, 'the film protected that little girl, Safa.' I touched my jacket pocket to make sure that Safa's letter was still there.

Joanna took a deep breath and quoted 'Whoever saves a single life earns as much merit as if he had saved the entire world. The Talmud.' My eyes filled with tears.

Before Joanna could see them, I wrapped my arms around her tightly and kissed her on the cheek. Then I let my tears fall.

Soulmates Joanna and Waris.

When we got to the hotel, I took off my jacket and fished the small sheet of folded, yellowing paper out of the inside pocket. I fell on to the huge, soft bed. I could hardly wait to scan the lines little Safa had written once more. As if she had read my mind, Joanna opened the laptop that she had set up on the desk in my room the day before.

'What are you doing?' I asked.

'I want to find the most recent photos from Djibouti that our representative there sent for you. There are some videos as well.'

Joanna set a box of material on my bedside table and put a DVD into the laptop. 'Waris, I'm dog-tired. I'm going to go to my room and call my son in Vienna before I go to sleep. I hope you'll be OK without me, but if you need any-thing else, give me a call.'

When she had pulled the door closed behind her, a smile spread over my face. Joanna, my soulmate, who had given me her support and advice as a manager and a friend for eleven years – I was hugely grateful to have her at my side. She was always ready to listen to my concerns, and always understanding when I made impulsive deci-sions, which were often quite inconvenient. Joanna grew up in Danzig, under Communism, but because her parents had rebelled against the regime, her family was poor and disadvantaged and Joanna had a difficult childhood. As a young woman she left Poland and went to university in Austria, where she also found a job. When she arrived, she didn't speak a word of German and had to survive by doing casual work until she learned the language. But she completed her degree, and soon became a successful businesswoman. Joanna's story reminded me of my time in London, when my relatives in the Somali Embassy treated me like a servant. When they left and I refused to go back with them, there followed a terrible period when I was living on the streets, unable to speak a word of English, when the only job I could get was as a cleaner at McDonald's.

Joanna knew what it was to be in a foreign country where she didn't speak the language, to get by without any help, overcome difficulties and never give up. These experiences bound us together without a doubt.

Sunk in thought, I slipped under the bedclothes, put the computer on my lap and started to click through the files. The first picture was of Safa's family. I immediately recognised the short, skinny man with the scrawny legs

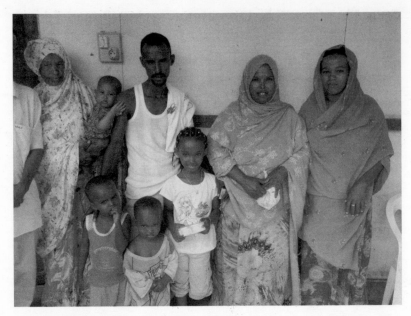

Safa's family, grandma Fatouma with baby cousin, brothers
Amir and Nour, father Idriss, mother Fozia and auntie Soraya.

and the serious expression as Safa's father. He had a
moustache and was displaying his yellow teeth. A thick
vein protruded from his forehead. His vest was only half
tucked into his washed-out trousers, the top button of
which was missing. Next to him stood Safa's mother, a
plump woman in a red hijab printed with white flowers, as
so many Somali women wear. Her almond-shaped eyes
gazed apprehensively into the camera, and she was wearing a faint smile. In her hands she held a package that I
had sent to Djibouti a few weeks previously. It contained
small pieces of jewellery made by a designer friend of
mine, which I had sent as presents for the women of the
family.

In front of their parents stood Safa's brothers Amir and
Nour, who at first glance anyone would think were twins.

Nour, the smaller of the two, was wearing a blue and white *Star Wars* T-shirt that was much too big for him, with CLONE TROOPER written on it. He was looking into the camera with a heart-warming shyness. Amir was wearing a ripped blue T-shirt with Arabic writing on it. Unlike his brother, he had a fierce expression on his face. And in the middle stood little Safa, beaming, just as I remembered her. She was holding a present from me – a little pink make-up box – with both hands. And from the necklace around her throat dangled the lucky charm that I had given her. It was the hand of Fatima, which was supposed to protect the little girl from evil.

*I'm so glad she's wearing the lucky charm*, I thought. I couldn't explain it, but looking at this group photo sent a cold shiver down my spine. Was it the old woman I didn't recognise who was affecting me like this? Was it her hostile gaze and the large, bony hands clutching the little body of a baby girl, who couldn't have been more than a year old? The longer I stared at the picture, the clearer it became: something wasn't right here. But what did this family have to hide?

I scoured all the other photos of Safa. The sweet girl with the big round eyes and the tousled black hair seemed cheerful and carefree in every shot. The other members of her family, by contrast, had scepticism and mistrust written all over their faces. But maybe I was mistaken; maybe they had just been frightened by the camera flash. The video waiting on my laptop would tell me for sure. Excitedly, I clicked on the 'play' symbol to start it.

Slowly, wobbling a little, the camera panned over the pale brown desert landscape. The light glistened on the African horizon I knew so well, where Djibouti borders

Somalia. The dull but stubborn pain in my heart came back every time I saw images like this. I had been leading a good, comfortable life in Europe for so long that it had become a second homeland for me, but my real home is the African desert. The older I get, the greater my longing for it. My parents had named me well: Waris means 'desert flower'. An abrupt change of shot interrupted my thoughts. Pink, turquoise, green: a huge collection of brightly painted corrugated-iron shacks now filled the screen. Fortresses of poverty, which offered people little more than a roof over their heads, shone in every colour. Unmade tracks snaked through the village between mountains of rubbish, stones, rubble and grey dust. The camera zoomed in on a rusty corrugated-iron fence that at some point had been painted blue. A small, shabby wooden door hung crookedly on makeshift hinges. From a ledge, a bored-looking little black and white goat was watching some children playing noisily in the dust by the fence. With a creak, the wooden door opened and a little girl came out, waving to the camera with a cheerful smile.

It was Safa, wearing an ankle-length dress patterned with pink and yellow flowers. Coloured beads bounced at the ends of her plaits. Yellow, red, blue and green, they shone in the sun like flowers in a spring meadow. Again my eyes were drawn straight to the glittering necklace she was wearing. The protective hand of Fatima lay in the hollow of her throat. I had to smile to myself when I spotted the gap in her otherwise gleaming white grin: it looked like Safa was starting to lose her milk teeth. The girl ran giggling towards a corrugated-iron shack, where a little broom was propped against the wall.

'I always make everything clean!' she cried proudly in

French, one of the two Djibouti languages, snatching up the old straw broom and sweeping the sandy floor enthusiastically, until she could hardly be seen in the cloud of dust she was stirring up.

'Safa, you're getting all dirty! We don't have enough water for me to keep washing you all the time.' Safa's mother sounded annoyed as she came into shot. When she spotted the camera, she laughed sheepishly.

The next shot showed the inside of the hut where Safa and her family lived. Its two tiny rooms, with their rough corrugated-iron walls and holed cardboard roof, were home to seven adults and five children. Safa and her mother sat down on one of the hut's two makeshift beds.

'How do people react to the fact that Safa is not circumcised?' I heard our representative ask from off camera.

'All the girls are circumcised here,' Safa's mother answered in Somali, our shared mother tongue, as she swatted at the flies that were settling on her little daughter's face. 'They are all circumcised apart from Safa,' she stressed again.

Wasn't she pleased that her daughter had been spared because of her film role and the resulting agreement, the interviewer asked.

'Yes, my husband and I signed this contract where we guaranteed not to have Safa circumcised,' the Somali woman replied. 'But to be honest I am not convinced that it was the right decision. The circumcision ritual is part of our tradition. We will never find a husband for Safa if she is not circumcised. She will never belong to our society like the other girls. So I am sure that one day we will have our daughter circumcised anyway.'

I couldn't breathe. What had that woman just said?

Had I misheard her?

I sat up suddenly and clicked on the stop button, to make sure I hadn't misunderstood Safa's mother. Could my Somali have grown as rusty as that after all these years in Europe?

'So I am sure that one day we will have our daughter circumcised anyway,' I heard the African woman say again.

With tears in my eyes, I watched as Safa nestled her head anxiously against her mother. The woman who not only wanted to break the contract she had made with my foundation, but was also prepared to sacrifice her child in cold blood for the sake of her reputation and the respect of the people she lived among.

My heart was racing. I was beside myself with disappointment and rage. What had been the point of all the conversations where my colleagues and I had explained to her in detail that circumcising women was a terrible crime – against her, me, all of us? What was the point of the contract that gave Safa's family financial security, a good education for the children and, with it, a better future? The Desert Flower Foundation had promised to pay for water, food, household goods, medical care and all education costs – but only if Safa was not circumcised.

The stone-cold announcement Safa's mother had made on camera brought all of this into question. Was circumcising her daughter really more important to this woman than the survival and future of her whole family? Evidently tradition was more powerful than any contract.

I glanced at the little clock on the bedside table. It was already late. All the same, I thought Joanna would understand, so I picked up the phone and dialled her extension. She whispered a sleepy 'Hello?' into the receiver.

'Joanna,' I said, so loudly that I could feel her jolt awake. 'I've just watched the video. We have to fly to Djibouti straight away and talk to Safa's parents.'

'How come? What's wrong?'

'In the interview, Safa's mother talks in Somali about wanting to get her daughter circumcised in spite of our contract. Joanna, we have to help the girl right now, before it's too late!'

'I'll go and check on flights now. There's no time to lose. ' Before I could say anything, she had hung up.

'I just hope we're not too late,' I said aloud to the empty room; then leapt up and prepared myself for the journey. I knew Joanna: she was sure to have us on the first flight to Djibouti City in the morning.

My suitcase was soon packed; the laptop which, less than half an hour before, had delivered the bad news from Safa's mother was back in its bag, and I was in bed.

It was pitch-dark in the room. I had pulled the thick, elegant curtains closed to shut out the bright lights of the Brussels streets. I had to try and get a few hours' sleep before we embarked. But thoughts about Safa were going round and round in my head. Was she all right? Might it already be too late? I tossed and turned in the soft bed until I finally fell asleep.

I can feel the heat of the sun on my skin. The water reflects the warm rays, which are making the surface of the sea sparkle a bright turquoise. The endless expanse of the Indian Ocean stretches out before us, and above it the sky is a radiant blue. The small, brightly painted fishing boat bobs on the water; glittering, foaming wavelets form around it before breaking and collapsing.

'Hey, Waris!' cries the young boatman, Ahmed. 'I'll drop you on the little island out there.'

With his finger he points to a silhouette looming on the horizon, over which a flock of birds is circling. I nod and take a deep breath of sea air.

'The island is uninhabited,' Ahmed explains. 'But there's an old, tumble-down shack where a fisherman used to live. He built it so he could stay overnight on the island if the sea was too stormy and he couldn't get back to the harbour with his catch. I'll take you there.'

Safa is sitting beside me on the boat's green-painted wooden seat. The wind is playing with her silky black hair, which has a reddish sheen in the sunlight. Her white dress flutters. The toddler from Djibouti's Balbala slums has turned into a beautiful little girl. Her white teeth gleam in the blazing sun. Beaming with joy, she holds tightly to a bracket on the boat's rusty roof. We are both squinting to get a better view of the solitary island in the distance. The warm salt water splashes into the boat and swirls around our ankles.

'Waris, I've never been in a boat on the sea. It's so beautiful here, I'd like to stay here for ever ... with you,' Safa shouts excitedly.

Then she shuts her eyes, as if she is trying to capture the moment. Softly, she starts to hum a song, though the melody is carried away by the wind.

Ahmed slows the engine and lets the boat bob gently towards the long white sandy beach. The beach is surrounded by a coral reef that looks like a huge wall built by an artist. I look around eagerly – and there is the tumble-down shack, standing on a little hill, just as Ahmed described it.

'I can't take you to the shore or the boat will get stuck in the sand,' Ahmed explains. 'You'll have to wade the last few metres.'

I climb over the old boat's rusty railing and jump into the sea. 'Now you. Don't worry, the water is lovely and warm,' I call up to the boat.

Without taking off her white dress, Safa leaps into the turquoise water. She soon surfaces again, spluttering and laughing.

I take her hand. 'Come on, baby girl, let's go to the beach.'

When we get to the shore, we pick our way carefully across the baking-hot sand covered in broken shells and dried seaweed.

'Come on,' I say, 'let's go to the old fisherman's hut. We can leave our clothes there.'

The furrowed door creaks loudly as I open it. Filled with curiosity, we step inside. The smell of sea and rotten fish greets us. Next to an old wooden table, which has almost rotted away in the heat and the salty sea air, stands a rusty bedstead, with the remains of a yellowing newspaper lying on it. Above the bed hangs a torn fishing-net. Sunlight comes in through the cracks in the planks of the walls. We hurriedly strip down to our bathing suits and run back to the sea. Safa bounds after me exuberantly. Little waves lap at the sand. Seagulls and crows search the shallow water for food.

'Come on, let's go further in,' I say to Safa. 'Out there, where it's deeper, we can lie on our backs and let ourselves drift. It's not difficult, especially not in salt water. The sea will hold us up.'

The warm waves swirl round our legs. When we reach the deeper water I stop.

'Now just lie flat on your back,' I tell Safa in a gentle voice. 'My hand will be under your back the whole time. Don't be afraid, nothing can happen to you. Trust me.'

Safa does what I tell her without any hesitation. I slip my right hand under her light body and the pretty girl floats like a little water lily.

Safa closes her eyes with a contented smile. 'I trust you, Waris.'

Her words give me goose-bumps in spite of the heat. I whisper softly into her ear: 'Sweetheart, I will hold you until you say you don't need me any more.'

When Safa opens her eyes again, the smile vanishes from her face. 'Look, Waris, what's that in the sky behind you?'

I turn around. A storm is brewing. 'It's probably going to rain,' I try to reassure her. 'But there's no need to be afraid. Water below us; water above us; water everywhere. It's a big party for us desert children.'

I have hardly finished speaking when a bolt of lightning flashes across the sky, quickly followed by a rumble of thunder that resounds over the ocean. Safa, who now has the ground under her feet again, opens her eyes wide in fear.

'I want to go back to the hut,' she begs. 'I don't want to stay in the sea. You can carry on swimming, but I'm getting out now.'

I let her go. While Safa makes her way across the sand to the shack, I swim over to the coral reef I saw from the boat. A stormy wind has blown up, and the waves are much higher than before. But I'm a good swimmer, and I love this kind of challenge. The storm hasn't quite reached us yet. Breathing deeply, I haul myself up to sit on a jutting rock and look towards the hut. Suddenly my heart begins to race wildly. Safa is not alone.

There is a woman wrapped in a long black robe with her, speaking to her and gesticulating. Who is this person, and where has she come from? Ahmed said the island was uninhabited!

'Safa! Safa!' I shout as loudly as I can. I wave both arms. Safa!'

But the howling of the wind, which is now growing stronger, swallows my frantic cries. Lightning flickers across the sky, and the thunder that follows rolls ominously towards us. The storm has reached the island and I am being whipped by the huge waves that have begun to crash against the rock where I am sitting. I decide that I will have to walk back to the beach along the reef. The razor-sharp coral cuts mercilessly into the soles of my feet. But I feel no pain. I carry on running, further, faster – always with my eyes fixed on the menacing woman who is now forcing Safa through the battered wooden door and into the shack. Finally I reach the end of the coral wall, and run up the beach to the shack. Panting, I pull at the door. It opened quite easily before, but now it's locked. I pound on the wood as hard as I can with both fists.

'Safa! Safa! Are you in there? Open the door!' I shout with all my might.

I hear Safa call for help. And then a shrill cry rings out.

I sat up with a jolt and rubbed my sweat-drenched face with both hands. I slowly opened my eyes, which were swollen and still filled with tears. My mobile was ringing on the bed-side table next to me. I reached for it as if in a trance.

'Waris! It's Joanna. I'm waiting for you in the breakfast room. Our plane leaves in three hours.'

# 2

# The contract

1 50kg sack basmati rice
1 50kg sack flour
1 10kg box pasta
1 5l can cooking oil
2kg black tea
50kg sugar
1 bottle tomato sauce
2.5kg dried milk
24 boxes biscuits
48 tins dried tuna
1 bottle washing-up liquid
1 box washing powder
Kerosene for two months + lighters
Additionally on the first delivery: 1 steam kettle

Quietly, Joanna read me the contract that my film's production company had drawn up with Safa's parents in

2007. We were sitting together on an Ethiopian Airlines jet, waiting for take-off.

'All of the above to be delivered at two-monthly intervals until Safa's eighteenth birthday,' my assistant read on. 'In addition, until she reaches her majority, the foundation will pay for all school fees, travel to and from school, school uniforms, schoolbooks, notebooks and papers, and a personal tutor. In return, Safa's parents promise that they will not allow their daughter to be subjected to genital mutilation. They also agree to have Safa examined by a paediatrician six times a year to check that she remains intact.'

I focused on the text in Joanna's hands as she sat beside me. Beneath the typed lines, the signatures of Fozia and Idriss Nour were large and clear. Safa's parents had negotiated the contract with Fardouza, the Desert Flower Foundation's representative in Djibouti, who also worked for the production company. In the presence of a notary, Safa's parents promised to keep her intact for ever. Another contract had been drawn up for little Idriss, the Somali boy who had played my younger brother (whom my family had always called 'Old Man'). His family, which consisted of three sisters and a half-blind father, had also agreed not to have the daughters mutilated.

I had been very involved in the casting for the film of my life. That was one of my conditions for agreeing to a film that would deal with the sensitive issue of FGM. The team searched New York, Los Angeles and Djibouti for suitable actors. It quickly became clear who should play me as an adult. Liya Kebede, an Ethiopian model, had already proved her talent as an actor in films such as *The Good Shepherd* with Matt Damon, Angelina Jolie and Robert De

Niro, and *Lord of War* with Nicolas Cage. She was a beautiful, talented woman and one of the world's most successful
models. The stunning Ethiopian already represented the
world's biggest brands: Gucci, Yves Saint Laurent, Louis
Vuitton, L'Oréal, Estée Lauder ... I was also impressed by
the fact that alongside her career on the catwalks of New
York, Paris and Milan, Liya worked as a special envoy to the
UN for the World Health Organisation.

Liya Kebede with Waris, supermodels and friends.

I had met Liya many years earlier, when I was still working as a model, at a party given by my friend and colleague
Iman, a model and the wife of David Bowie. I was at the
peak of my modelling career and had decided to give it up
in order to concentrate fully on my work as a human-rights
activist. In Iman's stylish New York apartment I noticed the
young woman watching me intently. After several hours,
she finally spoke to me.

'Waris, my name is Liya,' she began shyly. 'I've read everything about you and your work against FGM. I've seen all your photos. I only arrived in New York recently, to try and get started in the fashion industry here.'

When I finally said goodbye, wishing her luck, I never imagined our paths would cross again one day ten years later, when she would play the main role in my film.

Apart from the principal actors, one minor role lay particularly close to my heart: that of the little girl who would appear in the awful genital mutilation scene.

Nobody had ever made a feature film in Djibouti, and there were no professional actors there, so all the roles had to be played by amateurs. Our colleague Fardouza, a mother of five children, took on the task of organising and running the casting sessions.

Word of the film quickly spread through the capital city. Hundreds of parents from all over town arrived at the castings with their children. The women wore their prettiest hijabs, and had smartened up their children: nobody wanted to pass up the chance of getting a role in a big production, either to bring some change into their daily lives or in the hope of earning a little money and being able to improve things for themselves. This made it all the more difficult for the production team to choose their actors. But one thing was certain, they told me: they had to find a very special girl for the role of the young Waris. They wanted a self-aware little person with charm – a little desert flower.

Under the leadership of the fantastic director Sherry Hormann, the casting people saw dozens of toddlers. Many of them seemed terrified out of their wits, which made them completely unsuited to being in front of a camera. A few initially made a good impression, but none was really up to this demanding task. Within the team, there were discussions about whether to stop the casting sessions in Djibouti and bring in a professional actress from Europe or America.

Then one day a woman from the Balbala slums turned up with her two daughters, both of whom were cheerful little souls. She was holding another child in her arms, though she didn't say a word about her. The casting crew saw the older girls and talked to them for a few minutes, but it quickly became clear that neither of them was right for the little desert flower. As the disappointed young mother was turning to leave, Fardouza stopped her.

'Wait a second! Who is the little girl you're carrying?'

'This one? Oh, that's just Safa, my neighbour's daughter,' the woman said dismissively. 'I'm looking after her today, so I brought her with me.'

Fardouza looked into the lively eyes of the child, who laughed happily at her.

'Just a minute,' said Fardouza, trying to stop the woman leaving. 'We'd like to take a few photos of the little one.'

At that point, little Safa stretched out both arms towards Fardouza.

'Why don't you take one of my girls?' the woman snapped at her, holding her neighbour's daughter tightly. 'Safa is much too little. And her parents would never give their permission for her to be in the film. The family is very religious.'

Fardouza remained calm. 'Where does the girl's family live?' she asked in a soft, friendly voice. 'We'd like to ask the parents ourselves.'

'Oh, you'll have to go to Balbala,' the woman said. 'And I'm sure you know it can be very dangerous there.'

Desert Flower Casting, Djibouti, 2008. The first picture of Safa.

Fardouza instantly reached for her bag and put away the camera she had been using to take pictures of the candidates. The team would have to carry on without her for a while. She set off with the woman for the slums and Safa's family at once.

Balbala is the slum area of Djibouti City. As many as 400,000 people live there, crammed together under plastic sheeting or in tin shacks, most of them without running water or electricity. Even so, the poorest of the poor are better off here than in their homeland, Somalia, having fled under the most terrible of circumstances. Every year, the long civil war that is still raging in Djibouti's southern neighbour forces thousands of people to flee. And many more Somalis are forced to leave their homes during the country's frequent catastrophic droughts, to avoid dying of starvation, as hundreds of thousands of children and adults do every year.

The inhabitants of the Balbala slums all have one thing in common: they and their families have all come in search of a better life, never guessing how difficult things would be there. There is almost no work in the chaotic ghetto, which is not an official refugee camp. Clean drinking water is equally scarce, and the people live far below the poverty line. Child mortality is higher there than anywhere else in Djibouti. There are frequent periods of serious unrest, which regularly lead the authorities to block off the roads between Balbala and Djibouti City.

Where Fardouza was going was far from safe. She knew it wouldn't be an easy undertaking.

Reluctantly, the young woman who had brought Safa to the casting in the city showed Fardouza the shack where the girl's parents lived.

'Safa lives there. Good luck. I'm going home,' she said, before plonking Safa down on the dusty ground and leaving.

Disconcerted, Fardouza stood outside the shabby corrugated-iron house, from which a scrawny man with a moustache was now peering. It was Safa's father; he came out, gesticulating wildly at her.

'What do you want here? Go away!'

The child watched curiously with her large, dark eyes while Fardouza hastily explained to the man the reason for her visit.

'We would like to sign a contract with you. Your family will get a lot of money if you let your daughter act in our film,' she explained. She knew very well that she had to mention this right at the start.

The man gazed at his daughter thoughtfully, and she beamed back at him. 'Wait here!' A few minutes passed. Loud voices could be heard from inside the corrugated-iron hut. Then Safa's father suddenly came back and invited Fardouza into the house – this time very politely. On a wooden bench in one corner of the tiny room sat a stocky young woman who was obviously Safa's mother. Her name was Fozia and the father was Idriss. Fozia and the wizened old woman next to her did not look friendly. Fardouza saw at once that this woman must be Safa's grandmother. She knew that in Somali culture it is the grandmother who functions as the head of the family and has the final say in the house.

After a brief greeting, Safa's father came straight to the point. 'The first thing we want is plane tickets and a visa for France. And of course we'll need a lot of money.'

The family's extreme demands came as no surprise to Fardouza.

'I can barely feed my family; we often have nothing to eat for days on end,' Idriss explained. 'There's hardly ever any clean drinking water here. One of us is always getting sick. We can't afford a doctor or the hospital. I'd like to send my little boy to school, but we have no money for that. I'll never find any work here, and without work I can't look after my family.'

Slowly a conversation began between the family and the Desert Flower Foundation representative. Our organisation, as Fardouza explained to the sceptical adults, would ensure that in future Safa's whole family would be able to lead a better life. Of course, she added, the girl would appear in the film's pivotal scene – the circumcision scene – which would be entirely simulated.

'So, has Safa been circumcised already?' she asked cautiously, hoping the little girl would so far have been spared.

'No,' the father answered. 'But with the money we can finally afford to get her done. All the girls here are circumcised already, and it's a disgrace that our daughter is still running around unclean. People have started mocking us, and I'll never find my little Safa a husband who's prepared to pay a proper bride-price. And we really need the money.'

Fardouza was hurt by the man's words. She knew that people in Balbala practised 'pharaonic' circumcision, i.e. infibulation, the most severe form of genital mutilation. This procedure, which had also been performed on me many years before, involves removing the clitoris completely with no anaesthetic, often using a dirty old razor blade. Afterwards the labia are cut away, and the wound is closed using sharp thorns from a bush. Until the wound is healed, the girl has to remain lying down with her legs tied together. She is left with a single, tiny opening the size of a match head. Urine and, later, menstrual blood have to pass through this little hole. A huge number of girls die from the horrific procedure – if not from severe blood loss while they

are being cut, then of blood-poisoning, shock or an infection. Each girl who survives the cruel ritual will suffer
indescribable pain for the rest of her life. As if being mutilated in early childhood were not barbaric enough, the
husband to whom the girl's parents will one day give her will
cut open her scarred vagina with a sharp knife. For the
woman, the sexual act becomes a brutal, painful experience,
and the birth of each of her children puts her life in danger.
The mutilated vagina has lost its elasticity and can't stretch
far enough. It consists of dead tissue, and a scar through
which no child can enter the world easily. Many African
women die an agonising death in childbirth. The rest carry
the trauma of it with them for the rest of their lives.

Even so, these women will go on to do exactly the same
to their own daughters. They will bend to the pressure of
religion, tradition and culture, and carry their little girls to
the butcher's slab.

There was so much Fardouza wanted to say to Safa's
family at that moment. But she knew mere words were
redundant, and she would need a smarter plan to protect
this particular little girl.

Defeated, Fardouza returned to Djibouti City, where
she told Sherry Hormann and the rest of the team what the
tradition-conscious family had in mind. Then she called
me.

I was horrified. 'I will never allow a little girl to play that
role in my film, only to be mutilated for real afterwards!'

Sherry, Fardouza and I spent hours discussing how best
to proceed. Eventually, we came up with a solution that
would hopefully benefit everyone involved.

The next morning, Fardouza drove back to the slums of
Balbala.

'We've got a good offer for you,' was how she opened her second conversation with the girl's parents. 'If Safa acts in our film, we'll give you the chance of a better life. You'll never have to worry about your financial situation again. We'll give you a regular supply of food, water and everything else you need. Your children will go to school, and you'll be able to see a good doctor if any of you get sick.'

Fozia, Idriss and Safa's grandmother listened attentively to Fardouza's words.

Fardouza negotiates with Safa's family.

'You won't need to have Safa circumcised, or marry her off, because you will always have enough money,' she continued. 'And now for our one condition: you'll have to sign a contract with Desert Flower Film Productions GmbH, guaranteeing that Safa won't be circumcised, now or later. You will also give your consent for your daughter to be examined regularly by our paediatrician.'

When Fardouza looked into Safa's father's eyes, she knew he was already on her side. Of course Idriss, like almost any other African man, would never have married an uncircumcised girl. Still, he had no real opinion on the cruel ritual; he didn't see it as any of his business. In Africa, women take care of circumcision. His family's financial situation, on the other hand, *was* his problem.

But his wife shook her head angrily. 'Money is not so important to us. This is about preserving our traditions. If Safa is the only uncircumcised girl here, people will laugh at her!' She looked to the family elder for back-up.

All this time, Safa's grandmother had been sitting with her head bowed, not deigning to glance at Fardouza. Now she looked up for the first time, her eyes empty of expression. 'Go outside. I have to speak with my family.'

Fardouza stepped out of the shack and into the blazing sun. The hot wind blew the dust into her face. Would her plan work? Little Safa was squatting on a rock beside her black and white goat. Could this contract really save her?

After a few minutes, Idriss stuck his head out of the shack.

'Very well,' he said. 'We'll take your offer. We won't have Safa circumcised. But if the food is delivered late even once, we'll get her done!'

Fardouza told me later she wanted to hug him, but she was stopped by the piercing eyes of Safa's mother and grandmother, who now had stepped outside as well.

So instead she said, calmly but firmly: 'We've already made an appointment with the notary in Djibouti. We can go there right now and seal the deal.'

\*

Now, a few years later, I was sitting on a plane, on the way to Djibouti, my heart pounding with anxiety that the contract might have been broken. I couldn't tell if the rushing sound in my ears was the air-conditioning on the jumbo jet or my fear for little Safa. It would be awful if she had actually been forced to undergo that terrible scene we simulated so realistically on set.

When I looked over at Joanna I saw that her head was resting on the cabin wall, and she was breathing deeply. She had fallen asleep with exhaustion.

I reclined my seat and closed my eyes as well.

Two hours later we were woken by the clatter of meal trays. The attractive Ethiopian flight attendant served us drinks and dinner. Before take-off, I had noticed a few of them whispering to each other; but it was only now that one of the cabin crew actually addressed me.

'Miss Dirie, I'd like to tell you something,' she said politely. She bent right down to me and brought her face close to mine so that the passengers in the surrounding rows couldn't hear her. 'Three years ago I saw your film with my family in Addis Ababa. All the women at home are circumcised. After the film we had a long discussion about it, and about your message. Our men saw for the first time how horrific this ritual is.'

I nodded to her to continue.

The stewardess's dark eyes began to shine. 'We're so grateful for everything you're doing for women in Africa.' Then she reached down to her left wrist, where a colourful bracelet was dangling. 'I have a lucky band here I would like to give you.'

Before I could say anything, she had taken it off and was handing it to me.

'Please take it: it would make me very happy.'

She knotted the bracelet around my wrist and smiled.

The film had done more than I could ever have hoped. The flight attendant had no idea how much good her words had done me, just then, when I was so doubtful and afraid for little Safa.

# 3

# The film

For a long time I had resisted having *Desert Flower* turned into a film. After the book came out in 1998, several Hollywood producers got in touch with me, wanting to bring the story of my life to the big screen. I was presented with countless concepts, but all the pitches sounded the same: 'an African Cinderella'; 'from the desert to the catwalk'; 'the poor nomad girl becomes a supermodel'. None of these approaches convinced me. There was no question that my escape from the desert, my miserable life in London before the famous British photographer Terence Donovan discovered me working as a janitor in McDonald's and the fact that I finally became one of the highest-paid models in the world, was just the sort of material Hollywood blockbusters are made of. But it wasn't enough for me. Nobody wanted to tackle the part of my biography that was really important to me: FGM. Female genital mutilation wasn't exactly going to be a box-office hit in the glamorous dream factory that was Hollywood. They all wanted to film the story of my success, but nobody wanted to show the unimaginable horror that was part and parcel of my life. To many people's disbelief, I spent years turning down all the film offers.

Then one day I was approached by Elton John. I trusted him, and signed an option, a preliminary agreement with his film production company Rocket Productions. Elton personally saw to it that a screenplay was written in accordance with my ideas. He even invited me to his London mansion, where several writers were going to go over the script with me. Whether it was my sensitivity when it came to the taboo issue of FGM, or because there was simply no chemistry between me and the writers, the project foundered.

It was only some time later that I met the German producer Peter Hermann and the director Sherry Hormann, two people who were prepared to make a film about my life that didn't ignore the important issue of FGM. Sherry worked on the screenplay for months. Thanks to the empathy of everyone involved, and them allowing me a say in the matter, a film came into being that I could live with – no, live *for* – for the next few years.

When the movie was finished, the promotional tour began. There was no interview where I didn't have to talk about my own genital mutilation. No talk show where I wasn't asked about my sex life. Of course I realised it was important to raise awareness of the film and my battle against FGM all over the world. Even so, after some screenings I would sit in my hotel room and despair. I was torn between the knowledge that this work was necessary and the pain that burned in my soul when I had to reveal my innermost self to the public yet again. More than once, I toyed with the idea of simply running away: just leaving everything behind and starting a new, ordinary life somewhere else. But the countless emails and letters that the Desert Flower Foundation received after the film was released, and the generous feedback from people all over the world, were the encouragement and confirmation I needed to keep going.

The premiere in Ethiopia's capital city, Addis Ababa, was one of the high points of the trip. My mother, my brothers, and my nieces and nephews had all come from Somalia to see the film about their desert flower. I was particularly looking forward to being reunited with my mother. It was a long time since I'd seen her. And although I will associate her as long as I live with the terrible things that

Waris's family attend the Desert Flower premiere in 2010 in Addis Abada. From left to right: Waris's nephew Mohammed, her mother, her niece Hawo, Waris and her son Leon

happened in my childhood, my heart grew quite warm when she was finally standing in front of me again. In her long green dress and leather sandals, she looked as if she was one of the principal actors in my film.

Mama had hardly changed. She was still a simple woman who worked all day, took care of her grandchildren and tended the goats. But at our photo-call together for the Ethiopian press she surprised me. She looked so at ease, presenting herself as the nomad woman who had spent her life in the desert, far from civilisation. She posed beside me for the cameras with a smile and a twinkle in her eye, as if she had never done anything else. But that evening brought even greater surprises.

'Why would you show something like that?' my mother asked me, back at our hotel after the film première.

I knew at once what she meant.

A few hours before, I had looked over at her in the darkened cinema during the circumcision scene. I was trying to see what she was thinking, from the expression on her face as she watched this re-enactment of the torture she had witnessed somebody inflicting on me so many years previously. Would she be able to watch those horrific moments as coldly as she had then, when she pulled my legs apart behind a thorn bush to make the cutter-woman's work easier? No – to my astonishment, this time my mother shut her eyes, and even flinched at little Safa's piercing scream.

'Mama, you know exactly why we put that scene in the film. It's important for people to know what is being done to women.' As she removed her hijab thoughtfully and sat down on the sofa, I went on, without taking my eyes off her. 'I was watching you in the cinema. You closed your eyes during the mutilation scene. Even though the images were only made up and the reality is so much worse, you couldn't bear to watch it!'

My mother lowered her eyes in silence. At that moment, there was a lot more I wanted to get off my chest. And if she had told me, as she had years before, that I just didn't understand her, I might even have shouted and shaken her, to finally bring her to her senses. But just then there was a knock at the door.

The childminder who had been looking after my son during the première brought him in. Leon gave me one of his big smiles, and suddenly all my anger was forgotten.

'Mama, allow me to introduce Leon, my second son.' I held my baby out to her, full of pride.

My mother took the 'little lion', as I called him affectionately, and pressed a heartfelt kiss on to his cheek. She was clearly delighted that I was now the mother of two healthy boys.

When my first son Aleeke was born, I would have liked to share my happiness with her, but I was living far away in the USA, and after I separated from my partner, Aleeke stayed with his father. I simply wouldn't have been a good enough mother as a single parent. I was just beginning my battle against genital mutilation, which involved a lot of travel and an unconventional lifestyle. But now, my world looked very different. Now, my two sons were the most important things in my life, and my maternal duties fitted in with my work much better than they had in the years before.

'Such a sweet boy,' my mother beamed, hugging him tightly. 'You'll have to take good care of him.'

I knew exactly what she meant by that. She had long

cherished the hope that one day I would give up campaigning against FGM to concentrate on being a housewife and
mother.

My earlier anger began to seethe inside me again. Why
couldn't Mama understand that I would never lead a life
like hers, or give up my mission to emancipate African
women? I was despairing.

Her next remark caught me completely off guard.

'Waris,' she said, her voice beginning to waver, 'you
know I've brought your little niece Hawo with me from
Somalia.'

'Yes, I had a quick chat with her before the première.
What's wrong, Mama?' I asked hesitantly.

'You have to take her to Europe with you. Only you can
save her. Your sister-in-law wants to have her circumcised
very soon, and none of us at home will be able to stop her.'

I couldn't believe what I had just heard. My mother, who
had always defended the ritual and had argued with me
about it for years, was now trying to protect her grand-
daughter from being cut. Still holding little Leon in her
arms, she looked at me expectantly.

'Have you ... seriously ... changed your mind, Mama?'
I finally stammered.

My mother looked me straight in the eye and took a
deep breath. Then she said: 'Waris, what is done to the
girls is our tradition and our culture. Until a few years ago
I didn't even know there were women who weren't circumcised.'

I knew she was telling the truth. Many women, even in
my own generation and the one below, believe they share
their fate with every other woman in the world.

'And now,' she went on, 'I know people can live differently. Without suffering and without pain. And I am afraid for my grandchildren. So many girls die after they have been circumcised. I can't save Hawo myself. But you can! Please, Waris, take her with you.'

When my mother had gone to bed and Leon was asleep, I went out on to the little balcony of my hotel room. The starry sky glittered above the dark streets of Addis Ababa. Would I be able to convince my brother to let me take his two children? Because if I took Hawo I should also help her brother Mo in some way.

'One day I want to be just like you,' my niece had whispered in my ear after the screening.

I had explained to her that she must finish school first.

'Papa says we're going to run out of money soon,' Hawo had replied sadly. 'He lost his job as a security guard a few weeks ago.'

Only now, as I remembered that conversation, did I realise why my sister-in-law was in such a hurry to have Hawo circumcised. The girl's bride-price would provide for the family, at least for the next few months. No, I couldn't allow that. Hawo and Mo had to come to Europe with me.

And so, during one hot summer night in 2009 I went from a mother of two to a mother of four.

# 4

# Arrival in Djibouti

The hot desert wind greeted us at Djibouti Airport. I was still wearing my fur-lined winter boots, and had my violet padded jacket over my arm. I had put it on in Brussels without thinking, when Joanna and I were setting off on our urgent trip. Joanna had been in touch with Fardouza the night before, to tell her we were coming, but she hadn't been able to organise the necessary visas while we were still in Belgium. So we had to join the queue in the arrivals hall, where countless tourists were also waiting for their visas.

The oppressive heat inside the airport made beads of sweat stand out on our foreheads. I shifted impatiently from one foot to the other as we shuffled forwards along with everyone else.

Suddenly we heard an African customs official shouting: 'Hey, that's Waris Dirie, the famous model who made a film in Djibouti!'

I automatically pulled my cap further down over my eyes and pretended not to have heard him. But it was too late. Just a few moments later, Joanna and I were surrounded by five officials, peering at my face with great curiosity.

'Waris, sister, come with us. You don't have to wait here in the queue,' one of them said excitedly. 'For you, we'll make an exception. You must be here to make another film.'

I looked around in embarrassment. The tourists in the queue were staring enviously at us.

'No,' I replied awkwardly. 'I'm here to visit somebody. We've come to help a little girl in Djibouti.'

Before we knew what was happening, the officials had escorted us past the line of people and taken us into an office, where the door was shut behind us. An old air-conditioning unit on the wall rattled into life, to make the room at least a few degrees cooler. One after another, the officials left the room, leaving Joanna and me sitting on two clammy plastic chairs.

'What now?' I asked.

'I'm sure we'll get our visas any minute now. Then we can set off for Safa's house straight away,' Joanna said confidently.

We waited and waited. A good half-hour passed, and nothing happened. I began to get impatient.

'We could have stayed in the queue. We'd probably have been through customs by now,' I said, frustrated.

Joanna was just trying to reassure me when a customs official came in. He was not one of the friendly ones from before, but, as all the pips on his uniform told me, a manager who they must have sent for.

'What is going on here?' I asked angrily. I wasn't going to be intimidated by his stern gaze – I hadn't broken any laws. 'We've been travelling for fourteen hours, and I'm worn out.'

The official pulled up another plastic chair and sat down opposite us. 'Mme Dirie, are you aware that you need a work visa to enter the country?' he asked haughtily. 'You should have applied for it in Europe. As you did not do this, we must keep you here for the meantime, until we can clarify the situation, and organise a return flight to Europe for you if necessary.'

I was speechless. 'A work visa?' I cried furiously. 'What do I need a work visa for? I'm here in a private capacity.'

'But my colleagues said you were making another film here?'

Uncertainty spread across the official's face. Obviously embarrassed, he explained that the process for a tourist visa would take a little time, as the matter had been passed on to the office responsible for work visas, and must be cleared up there first. 'We will of course try to hurry things along, and you should be able to enter in twenty-four hours at the latest,' said the uniformed man generously.

Tired, desperate and angry at once, I sat there shaking my head. This couldn't be happening! I was stuck in a stifling hot airport building, wearing winter boots and a padded jacket, without permission to enter the country, and I couldn't even get changed as my luggage was waiting for me on the other side of customs. Joanna looked at me with helpless eyes, under which dark shadows had formed. I put an affectionate arm around her. I was sorry she had to go through all this with me, and that nothing ever went smoothly. But that was what working in Africa was like – always a challenge, always a battle.

Finally, after another hour of seemingly endless waiting, the border official came back. He handed me his phone. 'Here, this is my manager: he would like to speak with you personally.'

'Hello? This is Waris Dirie. I would like to enter the country as a private person – why are your officials making things so difficult for me?' I began, without waiting for a greeting from the man on the other end of the line.

Once again I was subjected to questioning about a film. I answered all his questions through gritted teeth, until he finally said, 'Mme Dirie, you may now pass through customs. We will have your visa brought to your hotel. But your passport will have to stay here until everything has been cleared up.'

I handed the phone back to the official in front of me, beckoned Joanna, and the two of us disappeared out of the door.

We had no more time to lose. It was already midday, and lessons would soon be over at Safa's school. Joanna and I wanted to go to collect her, so that we could speak to her alone. It felt like a miracle: we were hardly through customs and into the arrivals hall when we saw Fardouza, peering anxiously through the sliding doors. We had her incredible patience – and her knowledge of how drawn-out entry into this country could be – to thank for the fact that she had spent hours waiting for us in the heat.

To our surprise, our long-time supporter was not alone. At her side stood Linda Weil-Curiel, the Vice-President of the Desert Flower Foundation and a well-known human-rights lawyer from France, who had travelled from her Paris home. The border authorities here obviously hadn't given her any trouble, whereas my face was known and associated in Africa with my defiant battle for women's rights – a bad thing in the eyes of many people.

I hugged Linda warmly. I had long been impressed by her work for stricter laws against female genital mutilation. She had been the driving force behind the passing of a law that meant girls from African immigrant families in France had to be examined regularly to check they were still intact. The FGM laws in her country were more rigorous than anywhere else in the world. Linda had not only personally convicted several circumcisers in France and put them behind bars; she had also made sure the victims received compensation for their pain. Now this smart Frenchwoman was here to help us set up the Desert Flower Foundation in Djibouti.

'Quickly,' Fardouza interrupted us. 'We're late. Safa's going to be waiting for us at the school gates.'

In the baking heat we walked over to the car park, where a battered little grey Peugeot was waiting for us. Like most cars here, it had no air-conditioning. The heat in the car was unbearable, the air stifling and dry.

'Can I open the window?' I asked Fardouza, who was sitting beside me at the wheel.

'No!' she replied hastily.

But I had already pressed the button.

'You can't close them again: the mechanism is broken,' Fardouza muttered, pulling out of the parking space.

I closed my eyes and enjoyed the breeze. It was only later, when we hit the dust, that I realised why we should have kept the windows closed.

The airport wasn't far from the private French school that Safa attended. More than a thousand girls and boys from thirty different countries went there; it was very expensive so, like the other private schools in Djibouti, it only taught the children of diplomats, politicians and businessmen, most of them foreign. Safa was the exception – the only girl who was taken there every day from the slums of Balbala. Everyone in the school knew her unusual face, and had heard that she was a little film star.

When we pulled up outside the large white building marked ECOLE DE LA NATIVITÉ, people were already standing outside the gates. They were mostly parents, whose children were running to them, their schoolbags huge in comparison with their slight bodies. A few other pupils were making for large cars, where their chauffeurs opened the door for them with a flourish. It was lovely to watch all this cheerful activity, accompanied by the clamour of children's voices. As a mother, my heart at once began to beat faster in sympathy. I wondered how my little Leon, my niece Hawo and my nephew Mo were doing, even though I knew my children were in very good hands with their nanny, my close friend Senait, who was looking after the three of them at my house in Danzig. They were sure to understand why I had unexpectedly extended my trip, which should have just been two days in Brussels, to save another child. A child who was not growing up in such safety as they were.

A huge cloud of dust now hung over the school car park, stirred up by the procession of departing cars. Joanna, Fardouza and I got out of the Peugeot to look for Safa.

'I can't see her anywhere,' said Fardouza, her eyes narrowed to slits against the dust. 'I hope we haven't missed her.'

Linda had remained in the car and was coughing loudly. A cloud of sand had blown through the battered little car, settling on the dashboard and in Linda's lungs. I couldn't spot Safa on either side of the school fence, so I asked Linda, who was just clambering out of the car, to stay with it while I went looking for her. When Linda stood up, I had to let out a guffaw. The Frenchwoman was covered from head to toe in grey dust, and looked like a ghost. Coughing, she rubbed her eyes.

Still chuckling to myself, I walked into the school grounds and wove my way through the hordes of children streaming out of the building. I searched each pupil's face, hoping to see Safa. But she wasn't there.

Joanna and I were starting to get worried. Where was our little girl, the reason for our long journey? Slowly the school grounds and the street outside began to empty. It was getting quieter by the minute, as our shouts for Safa grew louder.

'Wait here for me,' Fardouza said finally. 'I'll go and find Safa's teacher. He'll probably know where the little one is.'

A short while later she returned with a perplexed expression on her face.

'What's going on?' I asked, unable to hide the tension in my voice.

'Safa left class with the other children,' she said. 'She's wearing a purple dress today. She wanted to look pretty for you.'

My eyes filled with tears of exhaustion, fear and desperation. 'She must be here somewhere,' I said to Joanna, when I had gathered my strength a little, but she just gave a baffled shrug.

Together we walked across the large playground, which was lined with eucalyptus trees to provide the children with shade in the baking heat. Some boys were playing basket-ball on an asphalt court. They hadn't seen Safa either. We walked quickly across the sports fields to the head's office, which was just about to close. The headmaster greeted us politely, but when we asked about Safa he had to disap-point us as well.

'Let's go to her classroom,' I said to Fardouza and Joanna.

We stood alone in the empty room, among the little desks and chairs where around thirty children usually sat. An old woman swathed in colourful robes muttered as she swept the floor. I let my gaze travel slowly around the walls, where dozens of the children's drawings had been put up. One picture immediately caught my eye: a pale brown beach in front of turquoise water, drawn with coloured pencils. I went closer to get a better look at the artwork. Only then did I spot the little hill on the beach, where the child had drawn a dark brown hut. I was instantly reminded of the terrible nightmare I had had in Brussels: it looked just like the beach where I had played with Safa in my dream. I took a step backwards in shock. And there really was a dark stormcloud above the hut, in the form of a wildly swirling scribble of black pencil.

I couldn't breathe. Was this an incredible coincidence, or was the picture some kind of sign from above, meant for me? I narrowed my eyes in an effort to decipher the tiny letters in the bottom right-hand corner. They spelled out *S a f a*.

I feared the worst. Had Safa run away? Or could her par-ents have something to do with her disappearance? That morning, Fardouza had told Fozia and Idriss that I was coming to Balbala to visit them. Perhaps Safa had already been cut, and I had arrived too late. Had my nightmare been an omen?

A tap on my shoulder brought me out of my reverie. 'I'll just get my mobile from the car and try to reach Safa's parents. Maybe they know where the little one's got to,' Fardouza said.

'I'll come with you,' I told her. At once I wanted to get out of the classroom, out of this empty room with my nightmare so ominously displayed on its wall.

Outside, I sat on a bench by the school gate with Joanna and buried my face in my hands. Thoughts whirled around my head. I was feeling worn out and disappointed.

'Waris! Waris! I know where Safa is!' Fardouza shouted, running across the playground towards us. 'Can you believe it?' she said when she reached us, out of breath. 'A school friend invited Safa to her birthday party. The girl's parents picked them up right after lessons. We probably only missed them by a few minutes.'

A stone weighing several tons fell from my heart. My little Safa was OK. But my joy soon turned to annoyance.

'How could the girl do that to us?' I said out loud. 'She knew we were coming today! We'll have to have a serious word with her.'

As fast as the battered – and now completely dust-covered – Peugeot could take us, we rattled through the streets of the city.

Djibouti City, the capital of the little state on the Gulf of Aden, is one of the most strategically important places in Africa. It lies on the 'Gate of Tears', a strait just a few kilometres wide between Africa and Asia, where the Indian Ocean meets the Red Sea. Every day, dozens of oil tankers from the Arab world, and cargo ships loaded with cars, electronic goods and textiles from Asia, have to navigate this passage. Whoever controls the strait controls the supply of energy to Europe.

Because of its position on the coast, Djibouti is also of great economic importance for its neighbour, Ethiopia. The only route supplying goods to Ethiopia, one of the largest nations in Africa, goes through Djibouti. Djibouti's other neighbours, Eritrea and Somalia, have been fighting a devastating civil war for years. This is not the least of the reasons that the USA and France have huge military bases in Djibouti, a tiny country of only around 9,000 square miles. The German Navy also has ships anchored there. Together, these troops keep watch over the airspace and the coast of East Africa, as well as the coast on the Arab side.

Djibouti is full of diplomats, secret-service agents, arms dealers and military officials from all over the world. Refugees from East Africa – men, women and children from Somalia, Eritrea, Ethiopia and Sudan – attempt to reach Asia and the rich Gulf states like Dubai and Qatar from here, in the hope of finding work and a better life. Unscrupulous gangs of people smugglers have made a booming business out of these people's misery. They cram hundreds of people into rusty old hulks and ship them from Djibouti to Yemen, in inhumane conditions. Many refugees die every year when the rickety boats sink, or when the smugglers simply throw them overboard into the ocean – after they have paid for their crossing, of course.

'Are there still pirate attacks here?' I asked Fardouza, who knew Djibouti like the back of her hand, as we drove past the mighty harbour. But my words were lost in the noise of the wind rushing past the car.

'What did you say, Waris?' Fardouza yelled, keeping her eyes on the road in an attempt to avoid writing off the car in one of the many potholes.

I leaned over to her. 'The soldiers. They're here to do something about the piracy, aren't they? Are they having any effect?' I said, trying to make myself heard over the noise.

About ten years previously, a series of brutal hijackings by Somali pirates had captured the world's attention. A lot of young fishermen from Somalia had been unable to resist the temptation of making a lot of money quickly on the high seas. Hunger had driven many of them to crime, because the big international fishing fleets had emptied the seas around Somalia of fish, threatening the livelihoods of all the small fishermen. Waste companies owned by the Italian mafia abused the coastal area that was left to the native fishermen, dumping their chemical waste there illegally. Fishing families who had sated their hunger with the contaminated catch succumbed to previously unseen diseases. Many died of cancer, and increasing numbers of children were born with deformities. So what did the fishermen have to lose? Piracy was their last hope of surviving and making money.

'I think so!' Fardouza shouted back. 'Since all these soldiers have been stationed here, there haven't been any more pirate attacks. The Gulf of Aden has actually got a lot more peaceful.'

Of course, that hadn't solved the problems of the Somali fishermen.

We soon reached Djibouti City's old town, which drove away the tiredness I was feeling after our long odyssey. I loved this area. Many of the French colonial-era buildings here retained some of their former grandeur, though they were crumbling forlornly, just waiting to collapse. But the markets were full of life, and I was delighted by the animated activity amongst the colourful stalls. Children, women, shouting market traders, shady street hawkers and beggars were all bustling through the narrow aisles between the colourful scarves, T-shirts, jewellery, fruit, grains, spices ... everything that there was to sell in this city.

Of course, a particularly lucrative business in these markets was selling khat, Africa's most popular everyday drug.

The khat shrub grows in the highlands of Ethiopia, and over the years has become the country's most significant export. Almost all men chew dried khat leaves for hours at a time, several times a day, to combat tiredness and, most importantly, hunger. A controlled substance in the United Kingdom, khat is legal in Djibouti, but interestingly, although women control the trade in the leaves, only men are permitted to consume the 'cocaine of Africa'.

We drove past many small groups of men who had settled down to chew in the shade of the city's few trees or on a dark street corner. I was saddened by their expressionless eyes: they reminded me of the circumstances that had driven these men to addiction. Khat allows people to forget their poverty, their fear, their worries and hardships. For most people there, khat is the only way to escape their misery.

'Is it true that a lot of children are taking khat as well?' Linda asked from the back seat.

'Yes, I'm afraid so,' Fardouza replied. 'The warlords in Somalia dole out khat to the child soldiers, to stop them being afraid of shooting and killing people.'

I said nothing. Who or what could ever save this continent from its hopeless situation? I certainly didn't have the answer.

'This must be it,' said Fardouza a moment later, pulling up in a side-street at the edge of the city.

We had finally arrived at the house where Safa's friend lived. There was a red gate set into a long, high wall topped with barbed wire.

Fardouza got out of the car and knocked. 'Hello!' she shouted. 'I'm Fardouza. I'm here to pick up Safa!'

While a young man let her in, I stayed in the car with Joanna and Linda. I imagined just what a telling-off I was going to give Safa for not waiting outside the school, and for making us worry so much. But my train of thought was derailed by the inquisitive gaze of the children who, within a few minutes, had surrounded the car. They had rushed over to find out who these people were in the dusty old banger. I had completely forgotten how curious people in Africa could be, how close they came to strangers, how they liked to touch and stare at them as if they were aliens. I decided to tease the crowd a little.

'Hey,' I shouted in Somali, getting out of the car. 'Don't you have anything better to do than stare at us?'

A few children shrank back in fright, but most of them stayed put and started asking questions eagerly.

'Are you Somali?' one little boy asked.

'Yes, of course, can't you tell by my voice?' I replied in my mother tongue.

'So why aren't you wearing a veil? Where's your hijab?' the cheeky boy went on.

'My hijab?' I replied haughtily. 'Why should I wear something like that? It's hot enough here as it is.'

By now a few grown men and women had joined the throng that surrounded me. They gaped at me in astonishment. I'll admit that I was enjoying their outrage. I knew that the men in particular were bothered by the fact that I wasn't veiled; it meant I was rebelling against their oppression.

As I was standing in the crowd, I suddenly felt one of the children nestling against me. A little hand reached for mine and squeezed it tenderly. To my surprise it was not one of the inquisitive neighbourhood children. It was Safa.

She looked up at me with her big, dark eyes and gave me an affectionate smile. 'Hello, Waris,' she said softly, resting her head against my arm.

'Go on, children, off you go and play,' I told the others.

I wanted to be alone with Safa. When they had gone, I knelt down in the sand and hugged her tightly. I had finally found her. At last I would be able to question her about her well-being myself – and protect her, with my life if necessary.

The moral lecture I had been preparing in the car was now completely forgotten. I looked into her almond-shaped brown eyes. Safa still held the same fascination for me as she had when Fardouza had introduced her to me for the first time. Then as now, I knew she was the right choice: gentle and warm-hearted, courageous and rebellious at once. Safa was like a mirror in which I saw myself as a young child. She knew exactly what she wanted. Just as I had done, she often drove her parents to their wits' end.

'Will you please behave like a girl and not like a bad boy,' my father scolded me more than once when I was little and had been on another one of my fearless expeditions through the desert. Even then, I hated long dresses and always hitched them up or tore them so I could move more easily and run faster. Now when I looked into Safa's eyes I saw my own untameable nature – which in the end had saved my life. Was I really going to scold her for this same quality that made her such a strong little girl?

Instead I decided to keep quiet and hold her in my arms.

# 5

# Safa's family

'I'd like you to sit next to me, Waris,' Safa said as we reached the Peugeot, where Fardouza was already sitting behind the wheel, ready to set off.

Linda and I swapped places so that Safa, beaming with delight, could sit between me and Joanna. I would have liked to take her straight to our hotel, to speak to the little one in peace about her letter, her worries and questions. I suggested this to the others.

'Sorry, Waris, we can't,' said Fardouza. 'Safa's parents are waiting for us. After all this time, they finally want to meet you – so we have to go to Balbala first.'

In spite of the scorching heat in the car, Safa snuggled up to me.

'Baby girl,' I said, my heart melting. 'Do you have any idea how much you mean to me? I've prayed for you so often. I wished so hard to see you again.'

Wordlessly, the girl pulled out the necklace that had

been hidden under the bright purple dress. She showed me the charm: the protective hand of Fatima, the necklace I had given her.

After a couple of miles we left Djibouti City and came to a bridge over the Ambuli River, which separates the city from the feared shanty-town of Balbala. Close by the over-populated ghetto stood an old lighthouse, which had given the quarter its name: *bal-bal* means 'to flash' in Somali. The tired old lighthouse was still doing its job, and so the people started calling the surrounding area Balbala. The settlement had originally been established as a French military base, protecting the city against insurgents. After Djibouti declared independence in 1977, the checkpoint had been removed, and the base turned into a residential area, where countless refugees from neighbouring countries had settled.

There was a military post on the bridge, below which the dirty brown water rolled sluggishly towards the sea. Safa climbed into my lap, clearly frightened of the heavily armed soldier who had stopped us. The uniformed African paced slowly around the car with a suspicious look on his face.

'What's going on here?' I asked Fardouza, who often came to this part of town.

'Waris, please don't say anything now!' she replied, giving the soldier a friendly smile. She whispered to me, 'There have been routine checks on all vehicles for a while now. After the elections we had terrible riots here, like many other African nations. The people didn't agree with the election results and they took to the streets. There was a lot of unrest, particularly here in Balbala. Cars were set on fire, and demonstrators blocked the streets and threw stones.'

A second soldier approached the car and stuck his head through one of the wide-open windows.

'Do you have any weapons?' he asked gruffly.

'No,' Fardouza replied. 'We're just taking this little girl to her parents in Balbala.'

The soldier's searching gaze travelled to Safa in the back seat, who was now pressing her face firmly into my belly.

'Drive on,' he instructed, letting us pass.

We crossed the bridge and reached the slums.

It was a shanty-town like hundreds of others in Africa, many of which I had seen. Through my work as a human-rights activist, I knew plenty of NGO workers who had spent years trying to help people in slums like this one. The problems in Balbala grew from one day to the next. Every day more refugees streamed into the settlement, which was estimated at roughly 80,000 inhabitants. Every day the conditions became more degrading. The lack of proper sanitation in slums frequently leads to epidemics. A lot of babies die before their first birthday because there is practically no medical care available. Hundreds of inhabitants suffer from chronic lung conditions, because the only way they can cook is on open fires in their tiny huts, and constantly breathing the toxic smoke makes them ill. Those who can afford a small stove cook with kerosene, which is no less toxic.

We could see at first glance that living conditions here were grim. We had hardly turned into one of the dirty alleyways between the corrugated-iron shacks when Fardouza had to stop the car: a woman was standing in the middle of the road, begging. From inside the length of cloth wrapped around her body, a baby was emitting heart-rending screams, probably due to hunger and thirst.

Fardouza sounded the horn in the hope that she would move aside, and the woman shuffled dejectedly towards the edge of the street.

I couldn't just sit there and do nothing. As Fardouza was about to set off again, I stopped her. 'No, wait!' I cried.

I rummaged in my small brown rucksack for some money before getting out of the car and slipping it into the young woman's hand. She thanked me with a tired smile.

Fardouza's Peugeot was instantly surrounded by mothers with babies in their arms; it was as if they had sprung from thin air. They too were in desperate need of money, and wailing for help. I couldn't stop myself: I hastily emptied my rucksack and divided whatever cash I could find among the women. Safa and the others in the car watched me.

Fardouza said with a laugh: 'You'll see, word of your generosity will get round in no time. Half of Balbala will be blocking the street on our way back.'

We drove on, up a bumpy unmade track between mountains of rubbish. Just when I was thinking there was no end to this street, Safa sat up in excitement.

'There, Waris!' she cried. 'I live up there!'

She leaned right out of the window, and the wind played with her dark hair. I was once again reminded of my nightmare, where the wind on the fishing boat had blown through Safa's hair.

'That's my *maman,* waiting out the front there,' Safa said proudly, pointing at a short, plump woman who was veiled from head to toe.

Fardouza parked between two wrecked cars and we got out. I went straight to Safa's mother, who I recognised at

once from the photo, and greeted her in Somali. Instinctively I held out both arms as if to embrace her, but the
Somali woman turned aside.

'I'm Waris,' I said, starting again. 'And what is your
name?'

The young woman looked mutely past me.

'Maman's name is Fozia,' Safa told me, grasping her
mother's hand. 'Come on, Waris! Papa, my brothers, my
grandmother and my uncles and aunts are waiting for
you.'

With that she grabbed my hand as well, and with a joyful
laugh dragged us both through the crooked wooden door
that I recognised from the video Joanna had given me in
Brussels. Fardouza, Linda and Joanna followed us along
the path into the dusty yard, where a long washing-line of
colourful clothes fluttered in the wind as if performing a
welcome dance for us. There was a little goat tethered to
a tree, being tormented by flies just as we were.

On the far side of the yard stood a small brick-built
house that was almost luxurious for this area, since it had
electricity and even a concrete veranda. I was surprised,
having expected the dilapidated shack that I had seen in
the video. Since then, thanks to our contract and the
support from the Desert Flower Foundation, Safa's
family had obviously been able to build a better house. I
was pleased at the progress, hoping it might have made
these people see sense and put them off breaking our
contract.

Safa's whole family was now gathering on the veranda of
the new house. More and more people came out of the
hut, lining up as if they were waiting for someone to take
a group photo. A scrawny man whom I recognised as Safa's

father positioned himself in the middle of them. He was proudly carrying his two sons, Amir and Nour, who eyed me with fierce expressions on their faces. Idriss, by contrast, smiled awkwardly and greeted me with a nod. The rest of the extended family just stared at me, silent and stony-faced.

'Hello, how lovely to meet you,' I said, a little hesitantly.

Joanna, Linda and Fardouza came to stand beside me, as if to lend me their support in this bizarre situation.

There was no reaction. Nobody returned my greeting.

Safa was still holding my hand, and she pulled me over to the little goat, which was resting in the shade of the tree. 'Waris, this is Ari, my goat. She's all mine. I find leftovers for her every day and bring her water.'

For a moment I forgot the hostile mob standing on the veranda. I bent down and stroked the animal. 'Did you know I used to have a lot of goats too, when I lived in the desert?' I said. 'It was my job to take care of them. Early in the morning I had to take them out to search for food, and I looked after them all by myself until we went back to our camp at sunset. My animals were the most precious thing I had. I love goats just as much as you do. I like them for their beautiful shiny coats, and because they're so strong-willed.'

As if to prove what I had just said, the goat bleated. Safa and I laughed heartily. I stood up and turned towards the girl's family, who were still rooted to the veranda, staring at me.

Finally Idriss gave the two boys to his wife and walked slowly over to me. 'How long will you stay in Djibouti?' he asked me, without offering any greeting. 'I have to speak to you alone.' Before I could answer, he went on: 'My family and I can't stay in Djibouti any more; you have to take us to Europe with you.'

Well, this was interesting. Not one member of the family had felt it necessary to greet me, or even to thank us for the support my Desert Flower Foundation had given them – and yet now I was supposed to take them all to Europe.

'I'm tired. Can we talk about it tomorrow please?' I wanted to put off the conversation, knowing it would not be an easy one.

'Yes – I'll come to your hotel tomorrow and we will talk about everything,' Idriss replied.

Safa was waiting impatiently to introduce me to her family. While the adults were still watching me sullenly, the girl dragged her brothers over to me. 'These are my two little brothers, Amir and Nour. In the afternoons when I've finished my homework, we play together outside. I always think up funny games. Shall we all play my favourite game together?' Safa suggested.

Since the rest of the family still showed no sign of speaking to me, I agreed.

We sat on the ground, and the four of us made a little circle. Safa started a version of a game that children play in Europe too. She called out excitedly in Somali, pointing at each of us in turn with her slender forefinger: 'Eeny, meeny, miney, mo – if I pick you, out you go. But you are not out so far, if you tell me how old you are.'

Her finger was pointing at Nour, the smaller of her two little brothers, who just looked at Safa blankly.

'Go on, Nour: you have to say how old you are,' Safa laughed.

But the funny little boy simply turned his head in shame and began to wail loudly.

Fozia hurried over and picked him up. As she did so, she threw Safa such a vicious look that even I was afraid.

'It's a shame you can't play it with the little one. He doesn't even know how old he is,' Safa explained to me, taking no notice of her mother. 'I tell him every time, so he can play. But when it's his turn he always just cries.'

With that, the game was over. We got up from the dirty ground and walked over to the veranda together, where Safa's family were still standing in a row. Fardouza and Linda stood a little way off, talking quietly to each other.

'Waris, this is my *maman*, Fozia – you know her already. This is Papa, his name is Idriss,' said Safa, pointing to each person with her tiny forefinger, as she had just done in the doomed counting game. 'Fatouma is my grandma. Over there are my two uncles, my aunts and my cousins. And this little baby here is my favourite cousin.' Safa confidently took a baby from her aunt's arms and presented her to me proudly.

'May I?' I asked the mother cautiously, looking down at this delightful child.

The woman signalled that I could hold her daughter with a subdued nod.

Under the whole family's watchful gaze, I lifted the baby above my head and back down, pressed my nose against hers and cuddled her. I love babies – these sweet little creatures who still have no idea what life has in store for them.

With Safa's cousin in my arms, I went back to Fozia. '*Assalamu alaikum*,' I said very politely, holding out my right hand to her in greeting.

She was short, probably not even five feet tall, and from her broad face I guessed she was very young. When she returned my greeting at this second attempt, I seized the opportunity and started up a conversation.

'Where does your family come from?' I asked her in Somali.

'Idriss was born in Djibouti, but I am originally from Ogaden,' Fozia replied.

'Ogaden – isn't that in Ethiopia? How did you come here to Djibouti?' I asked. I was glad that somebody was finally talking to me.

'We fled from the drought in our country. We lost everything. Our cattle, our land – nobody helped us. The Ethiopians didn't even allow the international aid transports to get through to us,' Safa's mother started to tell me.

I knew Ogaden had once been part of Somalia, before it was taken over by Ethiopia.

'Many of my family died, but my parents made it to Djibouti with us, when we were still children.' She went on to tell me about her mother and her husband, who was fourteen years older than her and had taken her as his bride when she was a girl of thirteen. Then she mentioned Safa, the first of her three children, who had been born soon after the marriage. 'In Ogaden there was plenty of space for us and our animals,' Fozia added with a note of sadness in her voice. 'But here we live among the poorest of the poor. It's hard, for all of us.'

'If you come from Ogaden, you must know Galkayo in Somalia as well?' I asked her.

'Of course: it's right on the border with Ethiopia,' Fozia said. 'We have relatives there. We belong to the Darod tribe.'

For a second I held my breath. Then I grasped Safa's mother's arm. 'I come from Galkayo, and I'm a Darod too.'

That broke the ice, and Fozia couldn't hold back any longer. She embraced me warmly, like a sister, pressing me to her.

'Come here,' she said to the others, who instantly gathered round us with curiosity.

All the adults began to talk at once, and a shower of voices rained down on me. Suddenly everyone wanted to know something about me or tell me something about themselves. Safa's aunt hurried into the house and came back with a jug of water and some beakers. Idriss fetched some chairs so that Joanna, Linda and Fardouza could sit down. Then Safa's grandmother Fatouma spoke up, and told us about the meaning of the little girl's name.

'Safa Idriss Nour, which is her full name, stands for clarity and purity,' explained the old woman, whose face was lined with deep wrinkles.

After a while I seized my chance, and said: 'You all know why I'm here. Our people have a terrible tradition: female genital mutilation.' In a second, everyone grew stony-faced. 'I am here to fight against it,' I said, carrying on regardless. 'Because this cruel ritual has one aim: the oppression of women. You have a wonderful daughter – Safa.' I gestured towards the girl we were sponsoring, who had gone back to her goat and was stroking it. 'I support her, which means I support you, too. The little one must never suffer something so horrific!'

The family lowered their eyes in embarrassment, as if I had said something indecent – something that people didn't talk about, weren't allowed to talk about.

'I'm going to stay in Djibouti for a few days, and I'd like to invite you all to a meal in my hotel, as a sign of friendship,' I said in an attempt to ease the tension. It worked:

the mood lifted at once, and we carried on chatting happily. Nobody else mentioned the issue of genital mutilation – for now, at least.

'Let's go back to the hotel now,' I said, a good hour later.

Tiredness was already etched on Fardouza and Linda's faces, and Joanna and I were especially weary after our long journey. My head ached, and I was worn out after all the problems we'd encountered that day.

'I really need to get some rest,' I explained.

Safa, standing next to her mother, looked at me with big, sad eyes. Fat tears rolled down her soft cheeks.

'Oh, baby girl, we'll see each other again tomorrow,' I said comfortingly.

But instead of cheering up, the little girl put her face in her hands and began to sob loudly. I went to her and picked her up.

'Why can't you stay with us?' asked Safa, her lip trembling. 'We've got room; you can sleep here with me.'

I explained calmly that it wasn't possible, and that I wanted some time to call my own children in Europe. 'They're missing me too, you know?' I said, trying to explain things in a way she would understand. No chance. She wrapped her slender arms around my neck, pressed her little mouth to my ear and sobbed: 'Waris, please take me with you. I want to stay with you.' Before I could utter another word, Safa turned to her father. 'Papa, can I go to the hotel with Waris and sleep there? Please?'

Idriss stared at me in surprise. It took him a few seconds to pull himself together. 'No, you're staying here. Your place is with your family,' he snapped at his daughter – but she wasn't giving up without a fight.

'But Papa, she's here for such a short time, and you can pick me up tomorrow morning. Or you can come with us now, and take me home again if you don't like it there.'

*Typical of my little fighter: she never says die*, I thought with a flutter of maternal pride, though without letting it show in my face.

Wordlessly Safa's father went over to Fatouma, who had been watching our debate from the veranda. After a brief exchange of words, he came back.

'OK, Safa – just this once you can spend the night with Waris in the hotel. But tomorrow morning you have to be ready for school at seven on the dot.' He raised a threatening finger to his daughter's face. 'And you, Waris,' he said, speaking to me just as sternly, 'you will please make sure that she isn't late. Please don't forget to give her a packed lunch. And now, Safa, go and get your schoolbooks from the house.'

The girl didn't lose a moment, charging over to her father and giving him a grateful hug.

Once Safa had rushed excitedly out of the house with her schoolbag on her back, looking as if she had never shed a tear, and taken leave of her suspicious family, we went back to Fardouza's Peugeot.

My three friends were already sitting in the car, waiting expectantly for the moment when we could finally be off. As I was trying to find room for Safa's satchel in the tightly packed boot, Idriss came marching out of the door to his humble property.

*What's the problem now?* I thought, disheartened. I was starting to lose patience. I just wanted to get out of there and drive to the hotel, where I could finally get a few hours' sleep.

'I've changed my mind,' Safa's father called out, heading for a rusty old vehicle that I had taken for a wreck when we arrived. 'I'm coming with you. I'll follow you. Safa, you're going in my car.'

But the little girl made no move to get out of the Peugeot, which she had climbed into as soon as she'd spotted her father.

'Oh, great,' I said quietly to myself, as I had took my seat in the car at last.

Joanna just gave me a tired, thoughtful look. She can't have imagined our trip would turn out like this.

Shortly after we left Balbala, when we were driving through a dangerous area, Safa's father overtook us. It was only thanks to Fardouza's quick reactions that we didn't plough into the back of the clapped-out yellow car. She slammed on the brakes, pitching us forward violently. Idriss dived out of his car, ran over to us and stuck his head through the open window.

'Hey, Waris,' he said casually. 'I totally forgot: do you happen to have a little money for me?'

I looked at Joanna in astonishment, and then back at him. 'But my foundation already supports your family; what could you possibly need?'

Idriss hesitated. 'Er, well . . . ' he stuttered. 'I need three thousand francs, actually. There's something I have to pay for.' Three thousand Djibouti francs was less than fifteen euros, but in this country it was a considerable sum of money.

'And I don't need to come to the hotel either, as long as you can help me out with this. I'll see you tomorrow,' he added hurriedly, when he saw the sceptical look on my face.

It was a reasonable price to pay to stop him accompanying us to the hotel. That meant I could spend a peaceful evening alone with Safa.

'Hmm. I gave all my cash to the women on the street,' I said, thinking aloud.

'And I've only got euros. I haven't had a chance to change any money yet,' said Joanna.

So I asked Linda to lend me the 3,000 francs for Idriss.

'Waris, you know very well what he needs that money for,' the Frenchwoman whispered to me from the front seat.

'Please just be quiet and give me the money,' I responded curtly. The tempting prospect of a few hours alone with my little Safa, and a chance to speak to her at length about her well-being, made me snap at her.

Linda said nothing as she reached into her bag, took out the money and started passing it to me. But before I could reach for it, Safa's father put his arm through the window and snatched the notes from her.

'Thanks – see you tomorrow then!' he called out cheerfully. He walked back to his car and sped away.

Linda turned to me again. 'You know very well he's not going to spend that money on his family. He's going to buy two days' worth of khat,' she said accusingly.

'Well then maybe he won't show up at the hotel until the day after tomorrow,' I laughed.

I knew Linda was right. Under normal circumstances there was no way I would have supported this man's drug habit, but at that moment the only thing that mattered to me was Safa's well-being.

The little girl snuggled up to me, beaming. That made it all worthwhile.

# 6

# In the luxury hotel

We drove along the coast road, and after a few miles turned off on to a peninsula. A narrow street led past the French Embassy to our hotel. The road was secured by military posts, and we had to keep stopping at barriers and showing our identification. At another stop, two security personnel politely asked us to open our suitcases and bags. They even searched Safa's brightly coloured schoolbag. Only then were we allowed to go on our way.

It was like taking a trip to another world. A manicured driveway led up to a huge, shining white complex of buildings. The hotel car park contained vehicles from international organisations and armed forces, with things like UN, INTERNATIONAL RED CROSS and GERMAN MILITARY POLICE written on their sides. Two doormen in elegant uniforms with gold name tags on their lapels were waiting in front of the revolving glass doors, to help us out of the

Peugeot and give us a friendly welcome. We climbed out of the car.

Safa, who was still wearing her purple dress, stared wide-eyed up at the hotel building. 'Wow!' she exclaimed.

I took her by the hand and we went into the spotless lobby, where more staff were lining up. The hotel manager hurried towards us, holding a bunch of flowers.

'Mme Dirie, it's an honour to have you here in our hotel,' he said, shaking my hand exuberantly and giving me the flowers.

I passed them to Safa, whose face disappeared almost completely behind the large, exotic blooms.

The hotel manager ushered us through the lobby to the lift. 'You don't need to check in at reception, Mme Dirie. We know who you are. May I take you to your room?'

I turned to my friends.

'We'll take care of the luggage, Waris,' said Joanna. As usual, she seemed to be able to read my mind. 'I'll see you in the café later on.'

We got into the lift. The manager pressed a button and the sliding doors closed quietly. Safa's little nose was peeping out between the blooms and leaves of the huge bunch of flowers, which she was still holding tightly with both hands.

'Waris, Waris,' she whispered in a frightened voice as the lift started to move. 'The room: it's moving. Are we flying now?'

I looked down at her and laughed. 'Yes, we're flying up to our room now – it's so far up, it's almost in the clouds. Here, give me the flowers and hold my hand.'

When we reached our floor, we stepped out of the lift. Safa stopped in front of it and put her right hand on her heart, looking as if she was completely out of breath. The hotel manager couldn't suppress a grin.

'Woah – a flying room. How does it work? Can we fly again please?' she marvelled.

'Safa, the flying room is called a lift. We're going to use it quite a lot in the next few days.'

`Please, please, let's fly again!' she begged.

'Not now. We're going to go to our room, but we'll have to go back down later, in any case.'

We walked a little way along the corridor, and then the hotel manager whipped out a magnetic card and opened the door to the room with a practised gesture.

Safa was beside herself with astonishment. 'What kind of magic trick was that?' she asked. 'Please show me how it works,' she said to the manager, who threw me an amused glance. 'May I have a go?' she said, and the kind man handed her the card and said goodbye.

'Safa, do you have schoolwork to do?' I asked her.

There was no answer. I turned around, but the room was empty. Then I saw the door open a crack and close again. Click, clack, click, clack, went the magnetic card as the little girl held it up to the locking mechanism again and again. I pulled the door open; Safa was standing in front of it with her new favourite game, and she looked up at me with big eyes.

'Safa, can you stop that please?' I said, slightly irritated. 'I'm really tired and I want to take a quick shower. While I'm doing that, you can do your homework.'

Hanging her head, Safa went to her satchel and reluctantly got out her books. She didn't look particularly happy about having to do schoolwork now.

'Listen, my little one,' I said gently. I was sorry for having taken a harsh tone with her. 'The hotel has a swimming pool. The quicker you finish your homework, the sooner we can go swimming,' I said in an attempt to cheer her up. 'I'd just like to freshen up and rest for a little while. As you can imagine, I'm very tired after the long journey.'

Safa sat down sulkily at the desk. I went into the bathroom and turned on the shower, which rained down a stream of clear, refreshing water. Splendid: that was exactly what I needed.

The cool water drove the tiredness from my bones at once. Refreshed, I came out of the bathroom to check on Safa. She had disappeared again. Worried, I scanned the room. Had she run away? This wayward little person was driving me mad! Then I opened the door into the hallway, where little Safa was once again standing with the magnetic card in her hand, blinking up at me guiltily.

'Safa, please,' I implored the girl. 'Sit back down at the desk and do your homework.'

'Waris, I was waiting for you.' This child was never in want of an excuse. 'I don't understand the questions. Can you help me?'

Although I had never been to school myself, as a single mother of two school-age children I was used to helping with homework. Without another word, I pulled a second chair up to the wooden desk, and Safa and I sat down. The girl read the first question aloud to me, and gave the right answer with a laugh. And then the second question, which she also answered straight away. She had no difficulties with the third either.

'Child, you don't need any help! You're doing these exercises quicker than I could!' I smiled.

The little girl laughed mischievously and packed the

books back into her satchel. She had just wanted to show me how much they had taught her at the school she was able to attend thanks to the Desert Flower Foundation's supporters. I hugged her proudly and gave her a kiss on the forehead.

As I had promised, I wanted to take Safa swimming.

'Oh dear, we didn't bring a swimming costume for you,' I suddenly realised. 'No matter, we'll pop down and buy one in the hotel shop.'

Safa looked at me quizzically. 'What *is* that: a swimming costume?' she asked, adding quickly: 'We go to the public beach sometimes, and I always swim in my clothes.'

'What? You can't swim in your clothes; you'll sink like a stone!' I laughed. I quickly slipped into my dark blue swimsuit, which Safa looked at curiously, pulled on a bathrobe and picked up a couple of towels. 'Come on, let's go down in the flying room and buy you your first swimming costume.'

Just as I'd thought, there was a brightly lit shop in the hotel lobby, selling souvenirs, cosmetics, clothes and swimsuits at ridiculously inflated prices. I took one swimming costume after another off the rail and showed them to Safa, but instead of picking one, she just wrinkled her nose.

'I want that one there!' she suddenly cried excitedly, running up to the shop window and pointing at a light blue one-piece with a giant Minnie Mouse on it.

It was the one of the most expensive suits in the shop, and the assistant hurried over delightedly and got it out.

'Try it on first,' I instructed Safa. 'I'll help you.'

This was my chance to go into the changing room with Safa. Maybe I could take a discreet glance at her vagina and find out whether the girl was still intact. The family's

hostile reaction to my words about female genital mutilation when we were in Balbala had only added to my
concern that Safa had already been cut.

'No, I can do it by myself,' said Safa, foiling my plans.
With that, she disappeared into the changing room and
pulled the curtain behind her with a mighty tug. I looked
worriedly at the wall of dark brown felt, hoping it wasn't
hiding what I was afraid of.

The swimming costume fitted perfectly. A few minutes
later she was proudly presenting the Minnie Mouse on her
belly to the handful of guests who had settled down on the
loungers by the long hotel pool. She posed in front of me
as if she was on the catwalk, planting her hands on her
hips and tossing her hair.

'Waris, do I look like a real model now?' she asked me
in great excitement.

She did actually seem to have the same natural talent
that had given me an international modelling career. I
never had to make an effort to learn or practise posing
and 'flirting with the camera', as they say in the modelling
business.

'Of course, Safa: you're a little desert flower, after all, and
all desert flowers are very beautiful,' I replied. I watched
her for a while longer, before saying, 'OK, that's enough
now,' interrupting her enthusiasm for a job whose rigours
this innocent child could not yet imagine. 'Let's get into
the water,' I suggested, standing on the edge of the pool.

Before I could turn round, Safa sprinted past me and
leapt into the pool without a second's hesitation. She surfaced again, coughing, and began to flail her arms wildly.
I saw at once that the little one couldn't swim properly. I
dived in after her. When I surfaced, I could see the little

desert flower paddling like a duck, coughing and snorting her way towards the side of the pool. With a few powerful strokes I swam after her and pulled her over to the ladder. Safa clutched it, laughing.

'Can't you swim?' I asked in a worried voice. 'You said you went to the beach with your family a lot.' I reproached myself for not having questioned her about it.

'What do you mean, swim?' the girl answered blithely. She was slightly out of breath. 'I know how to not sink, and how to keep myself above water,' she said with a laugh. Then she added: 'Can you show me how to do it properly, Waris?'

I promised to teach her to swim later; first, I wanted to take a minute and do a few lengths myself. I sat Safa on the top step of the ladder so she could watch me.

I pushed off hard with both legs, slid below the surface like a fish and enjoyed the cool water flowing over my body. There are only two kinds of exercise that make me feel really relaxed: running and swimming. Whenever and wherever I can, I put my running shoes on and go out. I have even run several marathons. Running and swimming both have something liberating about them. It's one of the reasons I had settled by the sea in Poland a few years previously. I felt free by the water. And now, in the comfortable temperature of the pool, I could feel how much good the swim was doing me.

Feeling relaxed and strong, I swam one length after another. After a while I turned on to my back, stretched both arms out behind me and opened my eyes to look at the sky. Suddenly, a dark shadow loomed over me from the side of the pool. It belonged to Safa's father, who was glaring at me angrily.

'How can you let my daughter run around almost naked with all these men here?' he screamed at me, while I swam to the side of the pool as fast as I could. 'She is a Muslim girl, and you know she's not allowed to show her body in public.'

I climbed out of the pool hastily and dried myself off, while he continued to give free rein to his anger.

'Even if I had allowed her to go swimming, she would have had to wear a long T-shirt and trousers. Not a bathing suit!' He put his hands to his head furiously. 'We are not in Europe, with the shameless unbelievers! I'm taking Safa back with me this instant!'

The little girl was hiding fearfully behind my legs. I turned to Idriss and glared back at him before saying in a quiet but firm voice: 'A few hours ago you were begging me to take you and your family with me to Europe.' My tone grew even sharper. 'I don't think we need to discuss that any more. It's better if you and your family stay here. After all, I wouldn't want you to have to live with the *shameless unbelievers*,' I added sarcastically.

The other hotel guests had laid aside their books and newspapers and were following our debate with interest. But I didn't care: they were welcome to hear me refusing to be oppressed, defending myself as I had done so often in my life. Idriss stared at me in astonishment, and then scratched his head. His daughter, who was still clutching my thigh, peered past me to watch her father's face. No woman had ever spoken to him like this.

After a while he cleared his throat. 'Er ... I actually came because my car broke down. It's a complete wreck. I have to get back to Balbala and I don't have the money for a taxi,' he finally ventured.

'But I gave you three thousand francs less than three hours ago. What did you do with it?' I asked – though of course I had a pretty good idea of what he had bought.

'Er ... I had a few bills to pay,' Idriss stuttered. 'I need another five hundred francs. My family is waiting for me in Balbala!'

Just then, Joanna came round the corner and headed towards us. She followed our argument with her mouth open in disbelief.

'And what's going to happen to Safa now?' I asked Idriss abruptly.

'Well, I *am* cross with you, but if she wants to, she can still spend the night here,' he said, relenting unexpectedly. 'I just need the money so I can get home.'

While I was still considering this, Joanna handed me the sum Idriss had demanded. 'Here, Waris, that's five hundred Djibouti francs. Just give it to him.'

Safa's father took the money, but made no move to leave.

'What now?' I hissed. Deep down I felt sorry for the man, because I knew only too well what poverty and hunger can do to people. But at that moment I was just fed up with him treating me like a cash cow.

'One more thing,' Idriss said, seizing the opportunity to make his next demand. 'I need a new car, quickly. Then I can work as a taxi driver and feed my family. I'm a really good driver,' he argued. 'I need a million francs by tomorrow, and then my friend will sell me his car. It's all agreed, and I can pick the car up tomorrow.'

I was pleased by the idea that this man would finally have work, and could stop filling his days by chewing khat. 'All right,' I said. 'Let's talk about it tomorrow.' I didn't have the strength to discuss it with him at that moment.

Dusk had begun to fall, and I just wanted to have something to eat and go to bed.

Safa picked up a towel and put it round her slender shoulders. She stayed by my side, looking at her father uncertainly. 'Do I have to come with you now?'

'No, you can stay here,' Idriss replied. 'But you must be waiting outside the hotel tomorrow morning at seven. I have to meet someone in the city, so I'll take you to school myself. You'd better be on time.'

I wondered what he was going to collect her in, if the clapped-out yellow car had broken down. But I didn't want to let the discussion boil over into an argument again, so I kept quiet. Idriss turned on his heel and left the hotel grounds, much to everyone's relief.

After a good dinner, I finally retired to my room with Safa. I called home and had a quick chat with my children, and then we went to bed. The little girl snuggled up to me and put her hand in mine.

'Thank you, Waris,' she sighed.

Before I could reply, she had fallen asleep with exhaustion. With my other hand I felt for my phone, which as always was on the bedside table. In the dark I wrote a text to Joanna:

We must take Safa to Dr Acina tomorrow. I want to make sure she's OK.

At seven o'clock the next morning I took a still-sleepy Safa to the hotel entrance. Her father was already waiting in the driveway in his worn-out, but apparently still drivable, car.

'Good-morning!' he warbled, clearly in the best of moods.

While Safa was getting into the back with her satchel, Idriss unexpectedly offered to let the girl spend another night with me at the hotel.

'Wonderful,' I agreed, showing myself to be equally cooperative. 'If you like, you and your family can come by this evening for dinner. I did promise you yesterday that I'd invite you to a friendship meal.'

Safa's father was delighted. 'We'll be there at six,' he said. Then he put his foot down and roared away, without giving me the chance to say goodbye to the little girl.

I watched the car drive away; Safa had turned round and was laughing and waving to me through the rear windscreen. Today was the day I would find out if she had really been spared the horrific circumcision ritual, as we had agreed with her family.

# 7

# A visit to the paediatrician

At exactly one o'clock, Fardouza, Joanna and I were standing in front of the large school building where we had
searched for Safa so desperately the day before. Today, the
girl came to meet us promptly as we had agreed. I had told
Safa that morning, as we were getting up, that we would be
going to see Dr Emma Acina, the girl's paediatrician. The
Desert Flower Foundation had an excellent working relationship with the doctor, who came from Madagascar and
was also active in the fight against FGM. We placed all our
trust in this woman. She had examined Safa regularly to
make sure she was still intact, each time confirming to our
relief that the girl had not been mutilated. Dr Acina also
took good care of Safa's brothers, immunising the boys
and giving them the necessary medicines when they were
ill.

Would she be able to reassure me again today that the
little girl we were sponsoring was still fine?

The atmosphere in the car was tense as we drove to the outpatient department in the centre of Djibouti City where the paediatrician had her practice.

When we pulled up in front of the building, a long queue of people was standing outside. Dozens of mothers had brought their children, some of whom were crying pitifully, to seek help from the experienced doctor. We had made an appointment, so Safa and I walked past the queue. Joanna and Fardouza said they would wait for us in a nearby café.

We climbed the narrow steps in the stifling, unlit stairwell, squeezing past more women and children who were waiting to be admitted. They looked at us in surprise. Dr Acina's receptionist was sitting behind a little desk on the far side of the overcrowded waiting room.

'Good-afternoon. I'm Waris Dirie, and this is Safa. My assistant called this morning to make an appointment for us,' I said by way of introduction.

The young woman gave me a startled look through her thick horn-rimmed spectacles, and stood up. 'Waris Dirie? Are you the author of *Desert Flower*?' she cried in astonishment, so loudly that everyone in the room could hear her.

Once again they all stared at me.

'Yes, that's me,' I said quietly while the African woman fished something out of her desk drawer.

'Mme Dirie, may I ask for your autograph?' she asked politely, holding out a pen and a French edition of the book.

I gladly signed it for her.

A few moments later, the door to the consulting room opened and Emma Acina came out. She was a short, plump woman whose smile I'd instantly fallen in love with when I had met her a few years previously. She greeted us warmly and ushered us into the consulting room, which looked very modern by African standards.

'You know why I'm here,' I began, having taken a seat opposite the doctor at the little desk.

Dr Acina nodded understandingly. 'This is about Safa, my favourite patient,' she replied, casting an affectionate glance at the little girl.

Desert Flower paediatrician Emma Acina in Djibouti regularly checks Safa.

Safa had found a stethoscope on the side table by the white examination couch. She had just put the earpieces into her ears, and was trying to listen to her own heartbeat with the other end.

'She comes here regularly, I can assure you of that,' Dr Acina went on. 'Safa is a healthy, lively and intelligent girl. And that isn't something you can take for granted here in Djibouti. Unfortunately, there are a lot of sick children here and not enough doctors to care for them all. I wish I could do more for the people here,' she sighed.

Dr Acina had an insight into the lives of people in every layer of society, so I asked her: 'Are you seeing a reduction in the number of victims of female genital mutilation?'

The paediatrician stared awkwardly down at her desk. 'The number of cases of *pharaonic* circumcision has fallen,' she answered honestly. 'However, the situation overall is still very depressing. The government is making a real effort, but there's been hardly any progress. They've stepped up the educational measures, but the ritual seems impossible to stamp out.' She explained to me that a law had been passed in Djibouti against performing FGM, but it was still only rarely enforced. 'It's difficult to throw ninety per cent of the population in jail,' she said resignedly. 'We still have a long, painful path ahead of us.'

Nobody knew that better than me. 'But as a doctor, you must have some influence with the people here. You must be able to explain the terrible consequences of genital mutilation in a way they'll believe,' I put in.

Safa had now come to sit on my lap, and was listening to us with rapt attention. I was glad she was following the conversation. Even if she didn't understand it all, it was important to speak frankly with her about this issue.

'Waris, you can't begin to imagine the awful injuries I see here every day,' Dr Acina continued, gazing sadly at Safa. 'Little girls with chronic inflammation of the vagina, bladder or kidneys. Girls with tumours the size of tennis balls growing on scar tissue that just keeps spreading. Young women unable to pass urine, and others whose mutilation has made them incontinent. Young children who can't get a wink of sleep because of the pain. Do you know how often I go home in the evening unable to sleep because of these images stuck in my head?'

I believed the doctor's every word. These conditions could unsettle even experienced, hard-bitten doctors.

'We can't give up, Emma,' I said encouragingly. 'If we don't fight it, who will? We need the support of everyone we can get, and you're right on the front line here.'

Having marshalled herself again, Dr Acina nodded, stood up and came over to me. She took Safa gently from my lap and turned to sit her on the examination couch. 'So then, young lady, we're going to examine you from head to toe now, to see if you're just as healthy as you were the last time you were here,' she said in a child-friendly voice.

'Are you frightened?' I asked Safa.

'No, Waris. Emma is really nice. And I want to be a paediatrician too, when I grow up. Then I can help all the children in Balbala.'

Smiling to myself, I left the consulting room, and waited outside for the results with a pounding heart.

'Everything's fine!' the paediatrician said as she opened the door, throwing me a reassuring glance.

Safa came out after her, ran to me and leapt joyfully

into my arms. 'Emma says I'm perfectly healthy,' she announced.

Dr Acina held out her hand in parting, but I instinctively hugged her, with Safa still in my arms. 'Thank you from the bottom of my heart. I was so afraid ...' I whispered into her ear.

'I know. But I'm glad to say that Safa's parents have stuck to the agreement,' the doctor said.

*For now, at least,* I thought as we left, watched by a lot of girls who had almost certainly not been as fortunate as my little Safa.

On the street I breathed in the hot air as deeply as I could, enjoying the sense of relief that Dr Acina had just given me.

'Safa, you know you can tell Dr Acina anything, don't you?' I knelt down to speak to the little one on her level. 'She's your friend and she'll always support you, whatever you need.'

Safa listened carefully, and looked at me with serious eyes. 'Yes, Waris, I understand. I don't want to be circumcised and get sick like those other girls in the waiting room,' the seven-year-old said, adding confidently: 'And I don't care if the other children laugh at me because of it.'

Giggling, we skipped through Djibouti's streets until we arrived at the café where Fardouza and Joanna were sitting in the sunshine. The two women gave me a worried look as we approached, but they could clearly see the relief on my face.

'Thank God!' Joanna gasped.

Fardouza balled her right hand into a fist and gave me a thumbs-up.

'Waris, I'm hungry. Can we get something to eat?' Safa asked quietly on the way to the hotel.

A few metres further on we spotted a fast-food place on the other side of the road. The giant hamburger on the sign attached to the roof of the little hut whetted my appetite, too.

'What would you say to a burger?' I asked Safa, who seemed to have no idea what I was talking about.

'What's that?'

I pointed to the sign on the building's roof.

'That's what a hamburger looks like. What do you think?'

Safa gazed wide-eyed at the advertising board with the bulging, larger-than-life white bread bun on it. 'No, I can't eat that much,' she sighed.

I laughed. 'OK, then, we can share one.'

We sat on the terrace and I ordered a burger with chips and ketchup. Safa was watching a man on the next table drinking from a can of Coca-Cola.

'Can I have one of those?' she begged.

I tried to explain that Coca-Cola was bad for her teeth and her body, but Safa insisted.

'Please, please – I never get to have it usually!'

How could I refuse this delightful child, who normally had to be content if her drinking water was reasonably clean? I caved in and ordered a can of Coke for Safa and an orange juice for me. A few minutes later the drinks and the burger were brought to our table. Safa gazed open-mouthed at the tower on the paper plate. 'It looks really good, but how am I supposed to eat it? Do you have to take it apart?'

Patiently I showed the girl something that came naturally to children in Europe or the USA. Safa opened her little mouth as wide as she could and bit into the burger.

'Oh no, now I've broken it,' she said sadly as half of the contents landed on the plate, the table and the floor.

'No, no, you can go ahead and eat the salad and the tomatoes with your hands. It tastes just as good,' I reassured her.

After a few bites, Safa had the burger under control and ate it skilfully. With her mouth full, she announced: 'From now on, I'm only going to eat burgers and drink Coca-Cola. They're so delicious.'

I had to laugh heartily again. Safa reminded me so much of the time shortly after I had come to England from Africa, when I worked as a cleaner in a fast-food restaurant. In addition to my wages, which were not worth mentioning, I got a free burger each day. For months on end all I ate every day was a single bread roll filled with meat, cheese, tomato and lettuce. But I didn't feel I was missing out; I still had no idea about the delicious food that existed outside the world of my childhood.

The day before, I had noticed that a lovely smooth path led along the coast behind the hotel complex. The sun was already low on the horizon, turning the sky red, and a gentle breeze was blowing off the sea, making the forty-two degree-air bearable. I hurriedly pulled on my running kit and my battered old trainers, and asked Fardouza to stay with Safa and help her with her homework. Before the girl's family arrived for dinner, I wanted an hour to myself, so I could go for a run towards the setting sun.

I jogged off at a leisurely pace, past the white seagulls fishing for crabs, mussels and leftovers in the bay, and the little heaps of rubbish washed up by the sea, from which startled stray dogs darted as I passed by. A few fishermen had already pulled their boats up out of the water and were panting as they cleaned them. A little further off, on a prettier part of the beach, some boys were playing a boisterous game of football in the sand.

I turned the volume of my iPod up full and picked up the pace. It was John Lee Hooker, with Van Morrison's song 'Gloria'. 'And her name is GLORIA, Gloria, Gloria.' I loved that song. I sang along enthusiastically, my feet pounding the soft, sandy ground in time with the music. One or another of the boys on the beach was sure to be staring at me in confusion – a singing female jogger was not exactly a common sight here – but I didn't care. As always when I was running, I was finally able to switch off and concentrate on the music, my rhythm, my breathing – leaving the past and the present behind me.

After a while I reached a particularly idyllic bay. I decided to take a little rest on the brightly painted fishing boat that was lying in the sand, solitary and abandoned. The setting sun caressed my face with its last powerful rays, and the wild evening waves raced across the surface of the sea and crashed on to the beach, breaking into foam. For a moment, the beauty of Africa, my home, made me forget this country's misery.

Suddenly a gigantic figure appeared on the beach. It approached at speed and finally came to a halt in front of me. It was a young, blond, muscular man in running gear.

'Hey, man, you're standing in my sun!' I joked.

'I'm sorry,' the runner replied in broken English. 'I just want to check if everything is OK with you. I thought maybe you collapse, because you sit here so alone.'

I didn't know if this was the truth or just a chat-up line, but I suddenly felt guilty about my abrupt greeting. 'Sorry,'

I said hurriedly. 'I was only joking. I'm fine, thank you. I was just enjoying this wonderful view.'

Relieved, my new acquaintance sat down beside me on the boat and held out a large, powerful hand. 'Hi. I am Jochen. I come from Hamburg.'

Only now that Jochen had stepped out of the sun could I see his face properly. With his large, dark eyes and thick blond hair that fell languidly over his forehead, he was a very attractive man.

'You look somehow familiar,' he said, as he eyed my face with a similar interest. 'It is possible we have met before? Where are you from?'

'Oh, well, from the same universe as you,' I answered flippantly, 'just from a different galaxy.'

That made him laugh. 'No, I think I know you from the television or so. Are you an actress?'

I shook my head and folded my arms over my chest, feeling embarrassed. 'No, I used to be a model. Now I'm an author and . . . ' I considered how best to explain my work to the young German without having to tell him my whole life story.

'Oh, you're the desert flower!' Jochen jumped in. 'The model from Africa who . . . ' Now he was lost for words as well. He seemed to have realised exactly who I was, and what had happened in my childhood. 'The model who was circumcised as a child; whose womanhood was taken away with a razor blade,' he might have been going to say. ' . . . Who is campaigning for years now against female genital mutilation,' he said, getting both of us out of an embarrassing situation.

Jochen looked into my eyes tenderly, as if he wanted to kiss away the pain from my soul. Then he flashed a sheepish smile and simply whispered, 'Waris. You're Waris Dirie.'

I felt flattered: a German jogger on a Djibouti beach recognised me and knew my life story.

'What are you doing here?' I asked him.

'I'm stationed here with the German Navy,' the man from Hamburg told me. 'We protect the cargo ships in Somali waters from pirates. Now and then we even catch a few of them.'

'That must be a dangerous job,' I said earnestly.

'No more dangerous than yours,' Jochen replied.

As it turned out, the German marine was staying in the same hotel as us.

'I'm running late already; I'm expecting guests this evening. Let's jog back together,' I suggested, and sprinted off.

'All right, let's go!' he laughed, and caught me up in a few metres.

It was a great feeling to run with somebody who was in such good shape. *And maybe it's a great feeling to run with a man who quite obviously likes you,* I thought to myself as we jogged along the coast in step with each other.

The men who came into my life had always fascinated me. Men I could laugh with, talk with, who I could even surrender myself to. Happily, both my sons were children born of love and passion. Even so, I was not made for conventional partnerships. The closer each bond became, the stronger my sense of anxiety and the feeling that I couldn't breathe. I could never put into words why it was. Perhaps it was my life history; the urge to be free that had been with me since childhood. Whatever it was, I was always running away. And I was running away again now, from any thoughts of flirting with an attractive young man.

'How long do you stay in Djibouti?' Jochen asked as we arrived sweating in the hotel lobby. 'I would really like to invite you to dinner.'

Without looking him in the eye, I ran to the lift, whose doors were just opening. 'I'm sure we'll see each other again. It was nice to meet you!' I called to him as I got in. Taken aback, Jochen remained standing in the hall, his lips pursed.

# 8

# The invitation

I leapt out of the shower, quickly towelled myself dry and pulled on my favourite jeans and a T-shirt. My long conversation with the German marine had made me late. Our guests had arrived and were waiting for me downstairs.

'Hurry up,' Joanna had told me twenty minutes before, when she had called my room. That afternoon, my friend and manager had decided to invite the little boy who had played my brother, 'Old Man', and his family to dinner as well. Like Safa's father, he answered to the name Idriss, and he lived in a village near the Somali border with his father and three sisters: Inab, Hibo and Hamda.

They had all come, Safa's parents had brought five-year-old Amir and three-year-old Nour, and the young Idriss was there with his father Abdillahi and his pretty sisters. Fardouza, Joanna and Linda had already taken their seats at the huge table beside the swimming pool, which was now a sparkling pale blue. At the head of the table sat little

Safa, who beckoned me over excitedly to the seat she had saved for me next to hers.

Unlike the previous day, the mood was relaxed from the outset. Fardouza, Joanna and Linda were talking animatedly to the father and sisters of young Idriss who, like Safa, had been picked for the film from the casting sessions in Djibouti. Beside me, Safa was excitedly telling her parents, brothers and fellow actor about everything that had happened over the last forty-eight hours. Whether it was coincidence, or Safa's natural diplomacy, to my relief the little one didn't mention our visit to Dr Acina. The issue would definitely have put a dampener on the mood once again.

A gigantic buffet had been laid out over five elegantly draped tables, which were literally sagging under the food. I was glad that today, at least, my guests could eat until they were full. Amir and Nour stared dumbfounded at the colourfully garnished food. At first, Idriss's two younger sisters just hid behind their pretty older sister Inab, not daring to take anything.

I had noticed Inab at once. She was an eighteen-year-old woman, but her eyes betrayed the fact that she had been through a lot in her young life. I decided to talk to Inab properly later on.

'Dig in – take what you want!' said Joanna, making a start herself.

Once they had got over their shyness in the face of the large buffet, our guests finally began to load food on to their plates. They served themselves eagerly, using their fingers, heaping different side dishes and mains on to the white china plates all at once. Meanwhile, the other hotel guests were queuing behind them, unable to get near the buffet. Indignant at the natives plundering the silver trays before them, they started clearing their throats and whispering to each other. I watched the activity in front of the buffet, amused and saddened at once by this lack of understanding from the luxury hotel's well-heeled guests.

Eventually everyone had more than enough on their plate, and we all sat down at the table.

'Do you eat meat at home very often?' I asked Safa, who was smacking her lips and peering out from behind a mountain of meat and French fries.

'No – only sometimes. And then it's mostly camel or mutton. Papa says Muslims aren't allowed to eat pork. And goat is just for special occasions, like a wedding or when somebody comes to visit,' Safa explained. She picked up a piece of chicken from her plate and ate it with her fingers, just as she had eaten the burger that afternoon. 'But I don't like to eat goat, because I don't want them to be killed. Nobody's allowed to kill my goat Ari, anyway,' she said solemnly. 'Ever, ever, ever!'

'And where do you get your drinking water?' I went on.

Safa's father, whose plate was already almost empty, answered: 'Mostly we buy it. There are a few wells in Balbala where the other families get their daily rations, but the water is very dirty,' he said. 'A lot of people get sick from it.'

Then Inab joined in: 'The water in the supermarket is really expensive. It's three hundred francs for a litre. Hardly anybody in Balbala can afford that.' Three hundred Djibouti francs was about one euro and thirty cents.

'My father used to earn twenty thousand francs as a security guard,' Inab said, answering my next question before I could ask it.

That was considerably less than a hundred euros a

month, for an entire family to live on. And on average, the bride-price a family received for a daughter who had been circumcised was equivalent to a month's salary.

When everyone was leaning back in their chairs, full and happy, Amir, Nour and Idriss went for a swim in the hotel pool. Never in their lives had they plunged into such clean, chlorinated water – let alone a pool that was lit up in the dark.

'Is Amir OK? He always looks so serious,' I asked his father, who was watching his sons with a smile of contentment.

'He is very sick,' Idriss replied quietly. 'Dr Acina says he has chronic bronchitis and severe asthma. He has to take strong medicine to stop him suffocating.'

Concerned, I asked whether the family could afford the medicines. 'Yes, thanks to your support we can buy him everything he needs,' the father of three replied, giving me a genuinely friendly look for the first time since I had arrived.

Inab told me that in her village, everyone knew about the Desert Flower Foundation and its work, and the neighbours often discussed my film. 'A lot of girls have been through the same thing as you; they've been cut too, but they refuse to accept that this ritual should continue. They would join the fight against FGM here if they could.'

Safa was listening intently to the eighteen-year-old, but the conversation about her people's traditions was clearly too much for the girl's mother. She stood up without saying a word and walked over to the pool to watch her sons playing. She probably didn't want to hear that even the neighbourhood children were starting to speak out against genital mutilation.

Inab wasn't put off by Fozia's reaction. 'It would be great if there was a Desert Flower Foundation office in Djibouti,' she suggested. 'I could work there, couldn't I? You know yourself how much work there is to do here. Apart from my sisters and Safa, I don't know a single girl who hasn't been circumcised.'

I wondered if I had heard her correctly. Inab had mentioned her sisters and Safa, not herself – which meant she had probably stared that horror in the face as well.

Then Safa joined in: 'Yes, it would be great if you had an office here, Waris! I could go there and meet other girls, and tell them how good it is to be healthy.'

I was astonished at the seven-year-old's maturity. But what would Safa's father think of his daughter, whom he wouldn't even allow to wear a bathing suit in the pool, becoming a living testimonial for the Desert Flower Foundation? To say nothing of his wife, who had seemed determined to break our contract at some point in the future.

But to my great surprise, Safa's father took a deep breath and said: 'The best thing would be to set up an office right in Balbala. I'd be happy for you to use my house.'

I was speechless. I stole a glance at Joanna, whose face had astonishment written all over it as well.

At that moment Safa's mother came back to the table with the three boys, who were sopping wet from the pool. I excused myself and walked through the hotel restaurant to the toilets.

Suddenly I heard soft footsteps behind me. It was Inab, who had followed me unnoticed. She gazed in awe at the elegant washroom, which was tiled in marble and hung with huge mirrors. A low bench with a red velvet seat stood in front of a make-up table. Inab sat down cautiously and stared at me, as if something was weighing on her mind.

'Is everything OK?' I asked.

'You know, Waris, I've been circumcised too,' said Inab, her eyes lowered in embarrassment.

I sat down beside her and gently lifted her chin with my forefinger, so she could look me in the eye again. 'You know that's nothing to be ashamed of,' I said. 'You're an incredibly brave girl who was lucky to survive this awful ritual. Just like me.'

Inab eyes filled with tears. 'But you managed to get out of here and make something of yourself. And now you're able to help a lot of other women. But I'm trapped here, powerless.'

I was touched by the words of the eighteen-year-old, who looked much younger than she was. 'You said before that you would like to help us. I'm very, very grateful for that, and together we'll find a way to grant your wish. Just give me a little time.'

With a sigh, Inab nodded and wiped away her tears. I knew that I had just taken responsibility for another girl's fate, and I fervently hoped I was up to this task as well. 'Right, I really do need the loo,' I said with a smile as I got up.

'Waris,' said Inab, holding me back. 'Do you get these terrible pains too? Sometimes I think I can't take it any more.'

I stopped breathing for a moment. I knew what Inab was talking about; I was only too familiar with the hellish torments that many women who had been mutilated suffered from all their lives.

'My child, I promise we will try to help you.' At that point, I didn't want to tell her that the only medical solution for her problem lay far away in Europe.

By the time Inab and I came back to the terrace, they were just serving coffee.

'Where have you been all this time?' Safa asked as I stirred my coffee thoughtfully.

I explained to her that I had been talking to Inab about the work of the Desert Flower Foundation. 'I am certain I want to work for you,' Inab said, seizing the opportunity to take up the subject again. 'Would it be possible to go to Europe and learn from you?'

Everyone stopped talking. Inab's father looked at me aghast. His daughter's direct question had taken me by surprise as well. 'Oh yes – I want to go to Europe too,' said her younger brother, breaking the silence.

Safa promptly chimed in too, but more quietly. 'May I come to Europe and do the training as well?'

Her father backed her up: 'Right. We all definitely have to go to Europe. If the people here knew we'd been there, they'd be much more likely to listen to us.'

The situation was now out of control. It was only natural that everyone who lived here in poverty wanted to get out of Africa. They all believed Europe was a fairy-tale land where there was no hardship. You just had to find a way to get there and all your problems would be solved at a stroke – that was the widely held opinion. And I was hardly going to be able to convince the people round the table that this was in no way true. So I just told them diplomatically: 'I'm afraid I can't invite you all to Europe.' Instead, I suggested arranging a trip to my new home continent for Safa and Inab – if their parents would allow it. Inab's father refrained from butting in, but Idriss did not.

'There's no way my daughter is travelling so far by herself. Either we all go, or nobody does.'

Safa lowered her head dejectedly and started to cry.

I decided not to let him shoot my good idea down in flames. 'Listen, Idriss. I'm sure you understand that I can't fly your entire family to Europe. But if you're genuinely interested in working for the Desert Flower Foundation, I'm happy to take you with us. But then you really have to do it – otherwise you'll pay back your travel costs.'

Stunned, Idriss stared into his coffee cup. Nobody said a word until Safa's father finally backed down. 'I could work as a driver for the organisation,' he suggested. 'And I'm sure I could convince some of the neighbours not to have their daughters circumcised.' He proudly added, 'We're a respected family in Balbala.'

'Wonderful,' I said, bringing the heated debate to an end. 'Idriss, Inab and Safa: the three of you will come to Europe for four weeks in the summer holidays. You'll visit Paris with the foundation first, then come to our office in Vienna.'

Safa's mother rolled her eyes. I could imagine what she thought of all this, and I hoped she wouldn't put a spanner in the works.

Meanwhile, Safa leapt up and started running exultantly round the table. 'We're going to Europe! We're going to Europe!' she shouted with delight.

I couldn't share her excitement: her mother's black look sent a cold shiver down my spine.

# 9

# A setback

Just before seven o'clock the next morning, Safa and I set off for school, on foot this time, as it was only a few minutes' walk from the hotel.

The previous evening, her parents and brothers, young Idriss's family and Inab had thanked us politely and said goodbye. I'd lain awake for a long time, still on a high from the productive conversations and the big plans we had made. Where were we going to go from here? Would I be able to protect Safa, who was lying beside me snoring quietly, for ever? How would we manage to free Inab from her terrible pain? Countless thoughts whirled around my head, not least the sad prospect of my imminent departure.

The fact that I had to leave Safa behind was already breaking my heart. But this cheerful little girl, who kissed me goodbye at the school gates, still had no idea about any of this.

I was hardly back inside the hotel before the manager

cornered me in the lobby. 'Dear Mme Dirie,' he said, 'I'd like to ask you a big favour.' I listened attentively to the Frenchman. 'This evening the hotel is hosting the annual gala dinner for the Djibouti Lions Club, and we would be delighted if you would join us as the guest of honour.' He paused, and then went on: 'You'll be certain to meet a lot of interesting people, who might be able to help you with your mission in Djibouti. There are several ministers coming, a lot of ambassadors, representatives from large organisations, and the heads of our international schools.'

This did sound interesting. Of course, while I was here I didn't want to waste a single opportunity. So I agreed on behalf of myself, Joanna, Fardouza and Linda.

I was just about to say goodbye when a young African woman in modern dress hurried up to the hotel manager. 'Excuse me, Mr Director: I've had all the new designs delivered, and I was wondering where my models can get ready this evening?'

'May I introduce you, ladies?' the manager interrupted the excited woman. 'Mme Dirie, this is Sagal, a successful fashion designer from Djibouti. She's going to present her new collection this evening. Sagal, this is . . .'

'Waris Dirie,' the designer interrupted. 'Of course I know who you are, I've heard a lot about you. African girls all dream of making it big in the fashion world like you did. Somali models are known throughout the world for their beauty. Which is a good thing; it means people don't just associate Somalia with pirates and this idiotic civil war. That's where I come from, too.' There was no stopping the young businesswoman once she had started talking. 'Waris, do you still model at all?' she asked.

I hesitated. I had bidden farewell to the catwalks of this world many years previously, and had turned down all offers of a comeback. The only time I appeared in front of a camera now was for an occasional charity shoot. I explained this, but Sagal assured me that a hundred percent of the income from tonight's show was going to the Djibouti Lions Club.

'The money supports state schools. Please walk tonight.' She looked at me with pleading eyes.

'Honestly, I really hadn't intended ever to set foot on a catwalk again. But then what wouldn't I do for a good cause and to support young talent?' I said, laughing. 'All right then, I'm in. But I won't go down the catwalk by myself.'

The designer looked at me quizzically.

'I'm going to bring someone with me. It's a surprise.'

Afterwards, over breakfast, I reflected on my short-notice acceptance of the fashion show, and on its lively organiser. I'd asked the hotel manager to tell me a little more about Sagal. As a young girl she had gone to Canada to study fashion design. Back in Africa, she had founded her own group of seamstresses to put her modern creations together. This meant she had developed a very special, unmistakable style, and – more importantly – she also created jobs for inventive young women, allowing them to become independent of their families and husbands.

Sagal's story gave me hope.

'Safa, I've got a surprise for you!'

I could hardly wait to tell the little girl about the exciting evening that lay ahead of us. I had waited impatiently for her outside the school, and now we were on our way back to the hotel together. 'If you like, you can walk down a catwalk with me today,' I said, eager to hear her reaction.

'What's a catwalk?' Safa asked.

I kept forgetting that this child had grown up in a completely different world, and had no idea about things that, over the years, had become totally normal to me. I described to Safa what I had in mind, and how we would present some beautiful clothes together that evening. There was just one condition: 'Only if you're not scared of getting up in front of all those people.'

As I suspected, the seven-year-old was far from shy. 'Now I'm a model just like you, Waris!' she cried happily. 'Maman and Papa have to see this. Can we invite them?'

I gave a start. I might have already persuaded Idriss to support me and the foundation in our fight against genital mutilation – and he might even accept his daughter modelling for a good cause. But the evil look that Fozia had given me last night still chilled me to the marrow. She certainly wouldn't want to see her daughter posing on a catwalk like a Western girl.

But how could I deny Safa's wish for her parents to see her first big appearance? How often had I longed for my family to be able to see me when I was celebrating my first successes as a model? There had been hundreds of people in the audience, and still I had felt alone.

When I got back to the hotel room, I called Fardouza. 'You have to do something for me,' I said to this good soul, who had been through so much with us over the past few days. I told her about the show that evening, and that I wanted to take Safa out on the catwalk with me. Without waiting for an answer, I went on: 'Oh yes – and the little

one would like her parents to be there. Could you invite
Fozia and Idriss please?'

'No problem, I can do that,' Fardouza assured me.

'What could we put Safa in?'

'Don't worry, Waris: I've got an idea,' Fardouza replied –
and with that, she hung up.

Twilight had descended over Djibouti. I stood at the
window of my room and looked down on to the terrace
where we had eaten the previous day with Safa and
young Idriss and their families. It looked very different
down there today. Uplighters were making the trees across
the hotel grounds glow in glorious colours. White spot-
lights made large, bright circles of light dance over the
turquoise water of the swimming pool. A red catwalk
stretched across the length of the pool, which was surrounded by hundreds of chairs and big, black speakers.
From where we stood, we could hear the thumping bass-
line of the music – there was obviously a sound check in
progress. Next to me, Safa pressed her little nose against
the window pane.

'We have to walk along that thing there?' she asked,
sounding nonplussed as she pointed at the catwalk, which
was tiny in comparison to international shows.

I tugged Safa's dress into place. Once again, Fardouza
had had a great idea. Like most girls in Balbala, Safa had
a Somali national costume, which Fardouza had collected
from the girl's parents and brought to the hotel. Now Safa
was standing in front of me in the robes her mother had
sewn for her, looking like a little warrior.

'You look great,' I said proudly.

I went and checked myself in the large mirror by the

door. Sagal had managed to find a dress that suited me perfectly. It was simple but elegant: flowing red material and a straightforward cut. *Fiery,* I thought, chuckling to myself.

Half an hour later, it was finally time. Joanna, who was helping Sagal with the fashion show's running order, gave me a quick call to say, 'Go.' It was something I had heard many times in my career.

'Safa, we're going to go down in the flying room now, and then we'll walk out together, OK?' I said, checking once again that Safa really wanted to do this.

'OK. What if I fall over?'

I could understand the girl's concerns – I used to have the same fears myself. 'Don't worry, you won't,' I reassured her. 'I'll be there, holding you tight.'

The frantic to-ing and fro-ing in the little room on the ground floor that had been turned into a wardrobe was the same as at big fashion shows all over the world. Wide-eyed, Safa watched the tall, slim models running around half-naked to grab the next outfit they had to present, then slipping into it and walking straight back out on to the cat-walk.

'Chop, chop – we have to move faster,' Sagal said, hurrying the girls along in time with the beat coming from outside.

The fashion show was in full swing. Around 150 guests invited by the Djibouti Lions Club had taken their seats on the terrace to look at the young designer's latest creations, and hopefully to hand over a lot of money for the city's public schools. Safa and I were the last item on the programme.

'You're the highlight of the show,' Sagal told us. The fact

that I wanted to take to the catwalk with the little girl I was sponsoring had made her even more enthusiastic. She knew this was a picture that was guaranteed to be all over the local media.

'Ladies and gentlemen, *mesdames et messieurs*,' I heard a voice say into the microphone outside.

Waris and Safa on the catwalk at the Sheraton Djibouti Hotel in 2013.

'This is it,' I whispered to Safa, taking her by the hand.

'We are delighted to introduce a surprise guest. Please welcome Waris Dirie!'

Hand in hand, Safa and I stepped into the light, where we were greeted by thunderous applause. As if we had practised it dozens of times, we walked along the red catwalk in perfect time to the music. When we arrived at the other end, we paused for a moment. Safa planted her hands on her hips, just as she had done two days previously in her new swimming costume, and beamed at the audience, whose admiration she was obviously enjoying. We walked back side by side – two desert flowers, one large, one small. It was wonderful for us both.

For the finale, the designer and all the models assembled on the catwalk to loud applause. The hotel manager hurried up with a microphone and thanked everyone who had taken part.

'Waris, thank you for doing us the honour this evening,' he said, turning to me. 'And please do tell us who the pretty young lady is you have brought with you.'

I took the microphone. 'This is my beloved Safa, who I am sponsoring. She played me in the film *Desert Flower.*' My gaze roamed over the rows of the audience. I finally spotted Idriss and Fozia right at the back, in a corner, sitting next to Linda and Fardouza. 'Safa played me in the horrific circumcision scene,' I said, looking at Safa's mother. 'The Desert Flower Foundation pledged to support Safa's family, in order to spare the girl from genital mutilation.' I wasn't sure how the guests, who included a lot of native politicians and opinion leaders, would react to my words. But to my surprise they all began to clap enthusiastically. 'It would be wonderful if you could tell as many people as possible out there about our work,' I went on, interrupting the applause. 'Tell the women and girls that it isn't necessary to suffer. That neither religion nor tradition demands or justifies this martyrdom that is inflicted on them. Go ahead and tell them about Safa: this healthy, happy, joyful little girl, who should become a role model for everyone.'

The audience showed their appreciation once more, but I kept my eyes on Idriss and Fozia.

After the show there were speeches from high-ranking members of the Lions Club, and then the guests took their seats at beautifully decorated round tables in the hotel restaurant. Safa and I sat next to the hotel manager and Sagal, who was in high spirits as she celebrated her success. Joanna, Fardouza, Linda and Safa's parents had been placed opposite us. Guests kept coming up to our table, saying hello to me and speaking a few kind words to Safa, who was over the moon at all the attention.

After dinner I went outside to take a break from the excitement and get a bit of fresh air. I stood underneath the arches beside the terrace, watching the staff dismantle the scene in which Safa and I had been. A dark figure suddenly appeared beside me. Safa's mother, as usual swathed in a traditional hijab, had followed me out. She stood for a few moments without speaking, obviously searching for words. I waited in silence, curious to hear what I was in for.

'Well, this is all well and good,' Fozia finally began in Somali, her dark eyes on me. 'But we both know that in a few days you'll be gone and things will go back to normal for all of us . . . Safa too. And normality, Waris, is no fairy tale like all this here.' She indicated the brightly illuminated garden with a sweeping gesture. 'Normality means we are increasingly becoming outsiders. We are shunned because we have an unclean, uncircumcised daughter. You are a Darod yourself.' The little woman tapped my chest with her forefinger. 'You know what happens to women who don't submit to the traditions. But you don't care about that; you don't live here. *You* ran away!' Fozia started to raise her voice. 'But we're still here, and we have to live with this shame that you have laid upon us! Safa is an outsider. In our village – everywhere. We are all outsiders.'

This wasn't the impression Idriss had given the day before. I tried to interrupt Safa's mother, but the rage that had been building inside her over the past few days was finally escaping, and it flooded over me like a giant wave, a tsunami of fear and desperation.

'I can tell you one thing, Waris,' Fozia went on angrily. 'My husband is on your side for now, because he thinks you're going to take him to Europe. But one day he'll realise he belongs here, and then he'll bend to his mother's will.'

I didn't understand her. 'Why are you blaming his mother? You want Safa to be circumcised too, don't you?' I said in a daze.

'Why do you think Fatouma is such a respected woman in Balbala?' Fozia said.

From far away, Safa's joyful voice reached my ears, which were buzzing with agitation. 'I've been looking for you two everywhere.' The girl looked curiously at her mother and me.

Fozia threw me a last angry glance, then took Safa by the hand, turned on her heel and went back into the restaurant with her daughter.

Stunned, I watched the two of them go. Had I understood what she was insinuating? Could Safa's own grandmother really be a cutter?

I had to get out of there. Away from the celebrating mob, who had applauded me earlier that evening – but what had they done to improve the situation in Djibouti? Most of the guests lived there and held important positions in the country, but over the last few years they had achieved almost nothing in the battle against FGM.

Alone on the beach in front of the hotel, I sat down on a low rock. The laughter, the music, the clatter and tinkle of cutlery and glasses – I wasn't really taking any of it in. The ominous silence of my battle, in which I had seldom felt so alone, stifled all the noise around me.

Suddenly a young man sat down next to me.

'Everything OK?' he asked. Jochen, the German marine who I had met on my run, sounded genuinely concerned.

This time I didn't joke the way I had the previous evening. 'Nothing is OK,' I said despondently.

'But your performance was fabulous,' he replied. He must have been in the audience at the fashion show as well, though I hadn't noticed him.

I didn't say anything.

'Is it something to do with the little girl who was with you?'

I looked over at him. Only now did I see he was wearing his uniform, and had gelled his blond hair back off his face. It made his features look even more angular; they somehow didn't fit with the tender look he was giving me.

'Her name is Safa,' I said after a while.

For a good half-hour the marine listened to me without

saying anything. I knew there was no advice he could give me.

'Waris, you come from Somalia yourself, don't you?' Jochen asked after a while. 'Do you have relatives there?'

'Yes. My mother, my father and my two brothers live near the town of Galkayo, not far from the Ethiopian border,' I told him.

Jochen looked at me. 'That's right in the middle of the civil war! Why don't you get them out?' He was amazed that I was worrying about a little girl in Djibouti, who was at least safe from the fighting, when I had left my own family behind in a war zone.

'I brought them to Europe a few years ago. I wanted so much to have them with me,' I told him. 'But their homesickness was stronger than their fear of the war. It broke my heart, but I had to let them go back to Somalia. Deep down, I understood. I often long for Africa, for my roots, for the desert.'

Jochen looked at me sympathetically. 'Africa is such a beautiful continent.'

'Unfortunately, it's a continent the rest of the world would rather forget about,' I replied. I stared thoughtfully out at the sea, which was hidden in the darkness. This wasn't news to Jochen: as a soldier, he knew what the issues were here.

'Waris, you can't pay every family not to have their children cut. And you can't save all the women in Africa on your own. You need the support of many, many people. And you need a good plan.'

Jochen was right. We had already achieved so much with the Desert Flower Foundation, drawing the world's attention to the issue of FGM. Now we had to make use of that attention. And my last appearance in Brussels had proved that I couldn't just rely on support from politicians.

Once again, Safa appeared in front of me as if from nowhere. 'Waris, come back inside. The party is so lovely,' she begged me impatiently.

The German marine stood up. 'Yes, have a lovely evening with the little one. I'm going to bed. We're sailing early tomorrow morning.'

It made me sad to think I would probably be saying goodbye to Jochen for ever. I got up from the rock and hugged him.

'I wish you all the best,' he said seriously. 'I know you will achieve what you've set out to do. And you, little desert flower,' he said, bending down to Safa and pinching her cheek affectionately as she gazed up at him, 'stay just as brave as you are. Africa needs girls like you.'

# 10

# A visit to Inab

The shrill sound of the telephone in my room jolted me awake the next morning.

'Hello?' I murmured sleepily into the receiver.

'*Bonjour, Waris!* It's Fardouza. Did you sleep well?'

I could only answer my colleague with a sullen growl. The events of the previous evening had made me so emotional that I had only managed to get to sleep just after two o'clock in the morning.

Fardouza was persistent. 'You know we're supposed to be going to Ali Sabieh today, to see Idriss, Inab, Hibo and Hamda. It's a fair way, and I expect there will be a lot of traffic on the roads, so we should set off as soon as we can.'

'What time is it?' I asked.

Fardouza was right: I was very keen to go to the remote village near the Ethiopian border, to visit Inab and Idriss's home. We were supporting their family as well, and it was important for me to see with my own eyes that the children were doing well.

'It's half-past four, and still dark outside,' Fardouza replied. 'We should really leave before sunrise; it's going to be very hot again today.'

'OK,' I said. 'When are you picking us up from the hotel? I have to take a shower, and I need a strong coffee before I go anywhere.'

The young woman gave me half an hour. The driver would be waiting for us at reception at five o'clock.

'OK, I'll be quick,' I groaned, forcing myself out from under the duvet.

Once the cold water had brought me to life, I shoved a few clothes into my rucksack to give to the children in Ali Sabieh, and quickly got dressed. I checked the time on my phone: it was exactly five o'clock, and the dawn was just starting to appear over the horizon. The sun would soon be up. I grabbed a bottle of water from the minibar on my way past, and was ready to go.

I started in fright as the door to the next room opened, and Joanna appeared in front of me with a rucksack.

Fardouza and our driver, Hussein, were already waiting. 'Off we go then, ladies,' said the African with a wide grin on his face, attempting to cheer us up as we trudged silently behind him out to his shabby 4x4.

'We never use the new vehicles when we're taking guests out into the desert,' Hussein said apologetically when he saw our sceptical expressions. 'All the dust, the sharp stones, the dry branches and the undergrowth just damage the cars. And we have to cross a stretch of real desert on the way to Ali Sabieh.'

'Oh, that doesn't matter,' I reassured him. 'The main thing is that we get there.'

'And back again,' Joanna laughed. 'How long are we going to be on the road?'

That would depend on the traffic, the driver explained to us, but he knew the area like the back of his hand. 'I worked for your organisation when you produced your film here. We drove out along that stretch every day – maybe you don't know that the desert scenes were all filmed along the road to Ali Sabieh,' Hussein said as we climbed up into the Jeep.

'Don't you want to sit in the front, Waris?' he asked me politely as I took my place on the back seat.

'No thank you, I'll stay back here with Fardouza,' I said. On my last day in Djibouti, I wanted to talk in Somali to our dedicated local representative. 'Joanna will keep you company; she soon starts feeling ill if she sits in the back.'

Hussein started the engine and pulled out of the hotel car park on to a narrow street that took us to a round-about. From there we turned on to the coast road. By this time, the sun had appeared above the horizon like a ball of red fire, making the Indian Ocean glitter in its morning rays. I watched the waves with a heavy heart. Tomorrow I would be going back to Europe and leaving all this behind.

A couple of miles down the road we passed the docks of Djibouti City, lined with warehouses and mighty oil tankers. As we drove up the hill, we could see the whole harbour and the Gulf of Aden. The cargo ships, as big as islands, the barges and the intimidating warships showed how significant the harbour was for the little country.

'Waris, do you see the mountains up ahead?' asked Hussein, who had stopped on the crest of a hill. I squinted.

'Across the sea there you can see Asia. The strait between Djibouti and Yemen is called the Gate of Tears. And we all know, whoever controls that strait has great power,' he said

Fardouza had already told me about this place, which was so strategically important to Djibouti and to the world. All the same, I listened to Hussein with interest. 'If either we or Yemen block the Gate of Tears, the lights will go out in Europe, and people will have to walk everywhere, because there'll be no more petrol.' The African laughed mischievously and looked at me in the rear-view mirror. 'Maybe that's why there are so many soldiers from all over the world stationed here. It's not because of the Somali pirates. The truth is there's much more at stake: getting energy to the West.'

'You know a lot about this,' I acknowledged.

He started the car again and went on: 'We are actually very powerful. If we started charging ships to pass through here, I'm pretty sure we wouldn't be one of the poorest countries in the world any more.'

'You should be a politician,' Fardouza remarked.

Joanna turned round to us and asked why the strait is called Gate of Tears.

'There have been pirates here for decades,' Fardouza replied. 'They've hijacked a lot of cargo ships, and sunk them. But the strait has more than earned its name now, because this is where the refugee boats set out from, full of people hoping for a better life. And, as I'm sure you know, many of them die because the boats are overcrowded, and they capsize.'

Joanna and I looked at Fardouza thoughtfully. Of course we knew about the refugee tragedies that play out off the coasts of Europe.

'You don't really see anything about them in the media here,' Fardouza went on. 'But people talk. A lot of people from East Africa, Somalia, Ethiopia, the Sudan and Eritrea are desperate to get away from their homelands. Some of them try and make it to Europe, but even more want to get to the Arab world. People dream of getting jobs in multi-billion-dollar paradises like Dubai, Qatar, Kuwait, Bahrain or Oman. The borders there aren't as secure as they are in Europe; the controls aren't as strict. Smugglers and gangs exploit the refugees mercilessly. They take everything from them, and they often end up killing them.'

Joanna's eyes opened wide. 'Isn't anything being done about it?'

Fardouza shook her head. 'There is no sympathetic authority in Yemen or Eritrea for the victims to turn to. A lot of people drown on the crossing, or they're killed. Countless young women end up in brothels or become victims of gang rape. There's practically nothing about it in the papers, but it happens every day.'

At this point our driver interrupted with a shake of his head. 'No African government has ever asked why their people are running away. So they don't care what happens to those who have fled.'

We reached an asphalt road where dozens of tankers and lorries were queueing, creeping into the desert at a snail's pace.

'Oh,' I groaned impatiently. 'How long is it going to take us to get to Ali Sabieh?'

'If it's like this all the way, it'll be tomorrow morning before we get there,' said Hussein, not giving me much hope. 'But I think the traffic will thin out in a couple of miles.'

In fact, the traffic soon started to move again, allowing Hussein to put his foot down at last. Our car rolled south towards Ethiopia and Somalia, towards home.

'Hussein,' I said, tapping him on the shoulder from the back seat, 'how far is it to the Somali border?'

'From Ali Sabieh you can go on foot and have a look at your homeland. The village is very close to the border between Somalia and Ethiopia.'

Metal shacks were scattered along the side of the road; between them stood rusted, gutted or burnt-out cars, ruined walls and heaps of rubbish. Sheer desolation. I closed my eyes and leaned back in my seat, overcome with doubt. *Why am I doing all this to myself?* I wondered. *To save a single girl from genital mutilation?*

Worldwide, 150 million women are affected by FGM. Thirty million girls are under acute threat in Africa alone, and I had come here to save just one of them – little Safa – in the continent's smallest and hottest country. I could just as well have chosen a girl in Kenya, a little Masai; a young Ethiopian; or one of the Egyptian girls who began to emancipate themselves in the Arab Spring, rebelling against the injustice they experienced every day.

But here I was in Djibouti. Most people don't even know where this country is. Once again I asked myself whether all the effort was really worth it. Could I justify saving this one girl, at whatever cost? Grappling with parents and authorities, with stubborn people who simply didn't want to change the way they thought. Could I have saved many more girls with the same effort in a different country?

My eyes closed with exhaustion.

A hand touched me gently on the shoulder and I woke with a start.

'Hey, Waris! Wake up,' I heard Fardouza saying.

'Are we in Ali Sabieh already?' I asked in confusion, rubbing my burning eyes.

'No, not yet,' Fardouza replied. 'But we're about to pass a special place. The place where that terrible scene with Safa was filmed.' I was suddenly wide awake. 'I thought you might want to see it. Just up ahead, round the next bend, there's an unmade track into the desert,' she explained.

'I'm not so sure,' I stammered uncertainly. 'Is it really a good idea to stop here? Maybe on the way back.'

Hussein looked into the rear-view mirror and said: 'It'll be too dark in the evening, and I'm not going down that gravel track then – the large stones are too dangerous. And there are a lot of holes we could get stuck in.'

I considered this. 'All right then,' I said finally. 'Let's stop for a minute.'

Hussein turned off the desert road. Tyre marks in the sand indicated a track, which Hussein followed. We were approaching a mountain range that shimmered blue in the blazing sun.

Twenty minutes later we reached our destination. Tufts of desert grass sprouted to the left and right of the tyre tracks, green harbingers of the vegetation that might one day colonise this place. We passed some large boulders and dried palms. The road was stony and the rain that pattered down here once a year had carved deep furrows into the sand. Hussein carefully manoeuvred the 4x4 through the obstacles.

'Up there, that's the place,' Hussein said, breaking the tense silence and pointing ahead.

He stopped and I opened the car door. As my feet touched the ground I could feel my knees go weak and give way, suddenly unable to carry my weight. My whole body rigid, I clutched the car door and looked straight ahead.

It was as though the film crew had only just left. I recognised the tree, the jagged rocks and the thorn bush. In my mind's eye I could see Safa, the old witch and the woman who had played my mother. I could hear the little girl's terrible cries. No: those weren't Safa's cries I was hearing – they were my own.

As I looked up, the rocks and the desert seemed to turn blood-red. I was still holding tightly to the car door. My stomach cramped as if it was being squeezed by a giant fist.

Then I felt Joanna's and Fardouza's supporting hands under my arms. 'Could you let me sit for a moment, please, on one of the rocks here,' I asked them. 'I just need to take some deep breaths.'

The two of them walked a few steps with me over to a rock where I could sit down. I took the scarf I was wearing around my neck and covered my head and face with it. I could still hear distant, high-pitched screams, mixed with the sounds of Somali dance music coming from the 4x4. The music distracted me from my harrowing thoughts, and I strained to make out the words of the chorus. 'I love you, my shining star; I love you, my blossoming flower; you are so pure, and you are mine.'

What a surreal moment! As I was painfully reliving the horrific mutilation scene, a young man was singing about stars, flowers and how he admired his 'pure beloved'. What a mockery! Millions of girls were being cruelly mutilated under the pretext of making them 'pure' – and here was somebody singing about 'love'. Sheer anger rose up inside me.

I decided to face up to the situation.

Grimly, I looked over at Joanna and Fardouza, who had gone to sit on another rock. The pivotal scene in my movie had been filmed on this exact spot. This small rock in the desert had become a place of dark enchantment. We all felt it: this spot, where I imagined I could hear Safa's shrill scream, had become the bleakest place in the world for us.

'I need to get out of here!'

Although I was whispering, Fardouza and Joanna seemed to hear me. They came over and walked me back to the car. Without a word, Hussein started the engine and made a U-turn. We were finally leaving this place of horror.

It was only when we had gone a couple of miles that I broke the awkward silence. 'Fardouza, why did you choose to film the scene there, over anywhere else in this big desert?' She looked out of the window, saying nothing.

I pressed her for an answer, sensing there was something our colleague wasn't telling me.

Only then did she say softly: 'OK, Waris ... when we were looking for suitable places to film, we asked the nomads in a nearby camp if they could recommend some-where. Then our Somali driver told us about this spot in the desert. People meet here to perform rituals. And ... they bring their girls here to have them circumcised.'

I was speechless. So it wasn't just the scene from the film that made that place feel so depressing – it was the fate of the girls who had experienced terrible things there.

Fardouza continued: 'When we came to look at the site, we felt just like you do now. But you won't believe what happened while we were filming.' She looked me straight in the eye. 'During a take, we suddenly heard a child screaming. Some of us dropped everything and ran over to see what was going on. ' Fardouza caught her breath for a moment. 'Two women were carrying a bleeding girl away. When they spotted us, they started running. Before we could do anything, they had disappeared. The rocks, the ground – everything was covered in blood.'

I could hardly believe what I was hearing. This was a place of darkness, despair and hopelessness. How many little girls had been tortured here, and destroyed for ever?

My mother had always told me that our God loved me. After I was mutilated, she said it was God's will.

I had replied: 'God can't love me; He must hate me, or He would never have let something like this happen.'

That made my mother very angry, and she walked away.

I spoke to God: 'You allowed this horrible thing to be done to me. Now You owe me something. If You exist, then let me live!'

Soon after, we passed some hills. The black volcanic rock turned the whole landscape a deep grey. By now it was boiling hot, and the air in the car was motionless. So this dark, dusty, sticky area was where little Idriss and his sisters had grown up.

We drove along a narrow, badly surfaced mountain road. Above us on the hill there was a rusted place sign with faded Arabic words on it, and underneath in Latin script: ALI SABIEH.

Ali Sabieh is one of twelve districts in Djibouti. Around 90,000 people live there in bitter poverty, on the border between three countries – Somalia, Ethiopia and Djibouti. The majority of them are nomads. There are hardly any jobs, and most people earn a little money by trading various goods. Anyone managing to get a job as a security guard – as Inab's father had – has reached the pinnacle of his career.

Inab and Idriss's father had been one of the lucky ones, until an eye problem cost him his job. It was a catastrophe for the family, who had managed to live a half-decent life on an income of around 20,000 Djibouti francs, or about eighty euros a month. Without the support of the Desert Flower Foundation, they might have starved after he was fired. When Inab was fourteen, her mother had abandoned her husband and four children. She just left – for no reason that would have been apparent to outsiders. Overnight Inab, the oldest, had to take over the running of the family home in Ali Sabieh. The way she took care of her little sisters Hibo and Hamda and her brother Idriss was really touching. Every day she got up at five and prepared breakfast for the whole family, before cleaning the shack and getting her little sisters dressed so she could take them to school. Then she set out to walk to her own school, a journey of over an hour.

The responsibility must have been a huge burden for the girl, who was not yet married, even though she had been circumcised. But Inab rose to the challenge that fate had given her. She got good grades, and protected her two sisters with her life. It was probably thanks to her that Hibo and Hamda had so far managed to escape genital mutilation.

As we approached the family's hut, I recognised Inab's sisters, Hamda and Hibo, from a distance. They were sitting on an old car tyre, drawing patterns on the dusty ground with stones.

'Inab!' they called excitedly when they spotted the car. 'Come out, Waris is here!'

We were hardly out of the car when the children ran up

Inab with her family in Ali Sabieh, Djibouti.

to us, beaming with joy, and threw their arms around Joanna, Fardouza and me.

The family had known Fardouza for years. She always made sure that the deliveries of food and kerosene that the Desert Flower Foundation had pledged to send to the children until they reached adulthood arrived on time. She also managed the school fees that the foundation paid. With no mother, and a practically blind father, Idriss, Inab, Hibo and Hamda had nobody else to rely on.

At this moment I also realised how important Fardouza's affection for the children was. Hibo and Hamda were clinging to her legs like little koala bears.

'May I show you our home?' Idriss said, turning to me, while Inab pulled me impatiently by the arm towards the shabby hut.

A mattress without pillows or covers lay on the floor, with a precarious-looking shelf that held a few books fixed to the wall above it. The hut had been cobbled together from stone, wood and cardboard, and a few sheets of cardboard and plastic formed the roof. Idriss proudly showed me his schoolbooks and his latest grades.

'Just look, Waris, in English I got eighteen point five out of twenty.' Lessons in Djibouti's schools were taught in French, so tests were marked using the French point system.

To my surprise, Idriss had his own little hut on the piece of land that their neighbours had let the family use. As one of the actors in *Desert Flower*, he was a kind of celebrity in the village.

'Come on, I want to show you our house now,' Inab urged me. The three girls had their own four walls as well, the sight of which shocked me, even as a native African.

This hut was constructed from cut-down, flattened petrol barrels, over which Inab had laid several plastic tarpaulins.

Inab led me into her 'empire', as she lovingly called it. This was where she and her siblings slept. The eighteen-year-old had piled their clothes in a corner, and their schoolbooks were lined up in an orderly row along the wall. Several brightly coloured cloths decorated the mattresses on the floor. The girls were obviously trying hard to make the best of their miserable situation, and to arrange their hut nicely.

'We did that all by ourselves, without any help,' Inab said, pleased that I had noticed their efforts.

'Waris, Can I make you some tea?' Hibo asked shyly, tugging at my shawl.

'Oh, that's very nice of you – you are a thoughtful girl,' I said, stroking one of her headscarf-covered cheeks. As soon as we arrived, I had noticed that Inab, Hamda and Hibo wore their veils even in their own home. 'Why don't you take your headscarves off? You're at home now,' I said.

The girls looked at me aghast.

'Waris, in Ali Sabieh all women have to wear a veil. Our religion demands it; even little girls go around in headscarves. You're not allowed to show your legs here, or wear trousers, let alone high heels. The people out there would kill you,' said Inab by way of explanation. The girl underlined the seriousness of the issue with a vehement gesture.

I couldn't stop myself: 'But we don't live in the Stone Age!' I exclaimed.

Even as a child I had hated the veil, and had earned several beatings for taking off my headscarf in public. A girl had to do what society expected, and cover herself up to stop men thinking dirty thoughts. In this part of the world, men even believed that women bore the sole responsibility for getting raped.

'Waris, as you know, I'm kind of a revolutionary here as it is,' Inab said in an attempt to justify herself. 'But even though I'm the oldest, my father doesn't like me leaving the house without my brother as a chaperon. I've often spoken out against circumcision, and everyone knows I stopped my little sisters being cut. Knowing about the Desert Flower Foundation has given me the courage to do it, because I know I'm not alone. But I'm afraid a lot of people here see me as a danger to their system.'

I listened to her, struck dumb with horror.

Inab told me she had once dared to go school without a headscarf. 'Even on the way there, little children were pointing their fingers at me. Well, I'm used to that. But then the adults started insulting me. "*Sharmuto* – whore," they shouted after me, and they even threw stones.' The eighteen-year-old gazed sadly at the ground. After this incident, she hadn't dared to leave the house for weeks. 'When my father heard about it, he was very angry. He screamed at me: "You're the only woman in the house; if they kill you, who's going to take care of the family? Who's going to cook for us, take the little ones to school, and keep up the connection with the Desert Flower Foundation that provides us with food?"'

I peered out of the hut, looking for Fardouza, but couldn't see her anywhere. There was no way we could tolerate this! Inab paused for a moment, and finally added quietly: 'My father didn't even consider that my brother, Idriss, who was already fifteen then, could have taken over those tasks. He's a man, after all.'

I listened closely to this graceful creature. She might be

small and thin, but she had a will of iron. One day, she would lead a better life. As soon as her sisters were old enough, she would go her own way and fight against the injustice being inflicted on women in Africa, I thought.

I put my arm around her shoulders and said: 'You're going to work for the Desert Flower Foundation; we're fighting for the same thing.'

The girl hugged me and laid her head on my chest. 'Thank you, Mama! But we have to start our work in Djibouti City. A lot of young, open-minded people live there, who we can reach more easily. When people here in the desert hear that the girls in the big city aren't being cut any more, it will set an example. At the end of the day, everyone wants the same thing: to get out of here, to the city.'

Suddenly Inab's brother, Idriss appeared in the doorway. The thin little boy had grown into a young man. His eyes glittered in the darkness of the hut.

'I don't want to go to Djibouti City. I want to go to Europe,' he said, interrupting our conversation. He was obviously having difficulty swallowing the fact that I had only invited his sister and Safa on this trip.

'And what exactly are you going to do there?' I asked him calmly. 'You haven't finished school yet; you haven't learned a trade. Do you think Europe's going to welcome you with open arms?'

Idriss just rolled his eyes and muttered: 'But I want to go to Europe! Please take me with you!'

I grew angry. 'Why do you want to go there so much? Who's put that idea in your head?'

He looked at me uncertainly. 'Well, in my school everyone wants to go to Europe. There are more than a thousand children and not one of them wants to stay here. What are we supposed to do here? There are no jobs for school leavers; even in the city, young people with degrees have hardly any chance of finding work. Should I just sit at the side of the road with all the others and chew khat?'

'No, of course not,' I replied. 'But you could work for the Desert Flower Foundation, just like Inab. We need everyone we can get here.'

Idriss lowered his head silently. Instead of considering my offer, he just repeated: 'I want to go to Europe, OK?'

This boy, who had given such a heart-warming performance as my late brother 'Old Man', seemed to be a hopeless case.

'Mama, your tea is ready,' came the chorus from the other hut. They brought me hot, steaming black tea in a battered aluminium container. 'We put lots of sugar in because it's a special day. It's really good now.' Hamda presented me proudly with their work.

Somalis like their tea very sweet, and I take mine with a little sugar and milk, too. But this tea tasted like a whole cup of sugar mixed with a little hot tea-water.

I took a cautious sip and praised the girls. 'Well done, thank you.'

Inab couldn't stop herself grinning – she knew the tea was as good as undrinkable.

Then her father came into the hut with our driver, Hussein.

'*Assalamu alaikum*,' he said and, without taking any further notice of me, sat down on a fruit box that served as a chair. 'Inab, I'm hungry. Make me something to eat,' he barked at his daughter.

The girl threw me an embarrassed glance, then took her

sister by the hand and hurried out of the hut. I followed her out and went back into Idriss's hut.

I took the opportunity to have a word with her father.

'We're supporting your family and you can't even greet me properly?' I snapped at him indignantly. I hated the way most African men treated women. As if we were second-, third- or fourth-class people. Abdillahi ignored my question. 'My son Idriss wants to go to Europe. When are you going to take him? He did act in your film, after all,' he grumbled instead, his tone hostile.

I was taken aback, but I remained patient. 'And what's your son supposed to do there? What do you have in mind?'

'Europe is incredibly rich. Just look at you: if a woman can do it, a man should have no problem,' he said cynically. 'We all want to send our sons to Europe, so they can send money back,' Abdillahi went on. 'Then if they do well, they can bring us to Europe too. The Europeans should be sharing their wealth with us – it's partly their fault we're poor in the first place. It's their duty to give us something.'

I struggled for words. 'That's the stupidest thing I've heard in a long time,' I said. 'People do well in Europe because they work. They have dreams and ideas that they put into action. The men there don't laze around day in, day out, chewing khat. The women are independent: they have their own jobs, their own income, and they know their rights. Don't you understand that Africa has to change? What use is it if you all run away?'

But like his son, he just repeated stubbornly: 'I want you to take Idriss to Europe.'

It was hopeless. I turned round without another word and left the hut.

Inab was outside, preparing food for her father.

'Could you bring me my rucksack with the clothes for the children?' I called out to Joanna, who was standing by the car, talking to Fardouza.

'I brought a few things for them as well,' she replied, fetching our bulging rucksacks from the car.

'Hey, I've got a surprise for you,' I called to the girls.

They stared wide-eyed as I pulled the clothes out of the bag. 'These are yours now.'

They danced around us, beaming with joy when they saw all the colourful material.

His sisters' excited squeals drew Idriss out of the hut. 'And what have you got for me?' asked the boy, whose envy was written large on his face.

Wordlessly I pulled out a T-shirt with the Eiffel tower printed on it and handed it to him. He eyed it critically, muttered something that sounded like 'Thanks,' and went back into the hut.

In the doorway he turned around and said stridently: 'I want a computer. Let's go and buy one now!'

Meanwhile, Inab was helping her sisters into their new clothes. They danced around the yard, laughing and twirling in their skirts and dresses. Inab tried on a red dress decorated with rhinestones, which she simply pulled on over her long-sleeved sweatshirt and skirt.

'You can't tell if it fits like that. Come with me and I'll show you how to try it on properly.' I took her by the hand and led her into the hut.

I instructed her to take off her clothes, and helped her into the dress. I looked around for a mirror, but there was none.

'How do I look?' Inab asked hesitantly.

What a shame she couldn't see herself in the pretty dress.

'I have an idea!' I cried. I got my phone out of my bag and took some photos of Inab to show her. 'You look so good you could easily become a model.'

Inab smiled proudly and asked me to take more photos of her in her new clothes. 'Maybe I really could become a model,' the girl wondered out loud. She tilted her head to one side thoughtfully and added: 'But I think I'd be better supporting you in your fight against FGM.'

We laughed and hugged one another. 'Thank you, Mama,' Inab whispered in my ear. 'I'll never forget you.'

We left the hut; outside, Hibo and Hamda were still admiring their new clothes.

Their brother stormed over to me in a rage and yelled, 'How come my sister gets to go to Europe? I'm the film star; *she's* just a girl. If she gets to go, then I'm coming too.'

I understood his anger – but for one thing Inab wanted to support me in my work, and for another she was old enough to take care of Safa, who would be travelling to Europe without her mother.

'Your sister is going to work with me,' I explained to him. 'She's going to learn from us. If you're prepared to work for our foundation, I will arrange for you to visit Europe too.'

I leaned in very close to his disappointed face, and took him by the hand. The boy couldn't help his petulant manner, but it would make life very difficult for him.

'Waris, we should head off before it gets dark,' Hussein pointed out. He had been chatting to the children's father. 'There's a lot of traffic around here in the late afternoon, lots of lorries taking the main road to Addis Ababa to get

their cargo on to the barges in time for it to be shipped.
They make the roads pretty congested.'

Inab gazed at me sadly. She knew it was time to say
adieu.

We took our leave from the families, and I put a loving
arm around the eighteen-year-old's shoulders as she
walked us to the car.

'Don't be sad,' I said, looking deep into her eyes. 'We'll
see each other again soon ... in Europe.'

Without saying another word, she hugged me tight.

'See you soon,' I whispered, and climbed into the car.

Hussein drove away. When I turned around to wave at
Inab, I saw her father callously grabbing her by the arm
and dragging her back into the hut. I knew we had to free
her from this misery as soon as possible.

The journey passed in silence, each of us dwelling on
our own thoughts.

'I want to see Safa again before we leave,' I said after a
while. 'Can we stop off in Balbala on the way back, please?'

Hussein shook his head. 'I'm sorry, but I'm strictly for-
bidden to drive there after dark. Nobody can guarantee
your safety at night – and in any case, it's not on the way
back to the hotel.'

'I don't care,' I retorted. 'I want to say goodbye to Safa.
I'm Somali; I'm not afraid!'

The usually friendly driver grew impatient. 'Yes, but
then I'll lose my job as a chauffeur, and I'm certainly not
going to risk that. Sorry!'

Fardouza, who could see my frustration, tried to bring
me round. 'Don't worry, Waris: I have a solution. I'll bring
Safa to the airport tomorrow morning, so you can say
goodbye. What do you think?'

It was a good compromise, and I agreed. It didn't matter where or when – I had to see my little desert flower again before we left.

The journey back went just as Hussein had said it would: we inched along through the traffic, only reaching the hotel just before midnight. Joanna and I had exactly three hours to rest before our alarms went off.

I was exhausted, but the thought of holding Safa in my arms again kept me going.

Joanna and I left the hotel at four the next morning. Hussein, who insisted on taking us to the airport personally, was already standing at the hotel entrance, and took our suitcases.

We drove along the badly lit coast road, with the full moon hanging low in the clear night sky and bathing our surroundings in its pale light.

Thirty minutes later I leapt out of the car at the airport doors, and looked around. There was no sign of Fardouza and Safa. Hussein unloaded our luggage and walked us to the Ethiopian Airlines desk, where Joanna and I checked in. We had our boarding cards, and could have gone through passport control. But where was my little desert flower? I paced fretfully up and down the small departures hall.

'Joanna, I can't leave without saying goodbye to Safa,' I said after a while. My manager was already looking impatiently at her watch.

She got her phone out of her bag, dialled Fardouza's number and held it to my ear.

'The number you have dialled is not available, please try again later,' said a monotonous recorded voice.

'Please let's go to the entrance again. Maybe they're just parking,' I begged my companion. Two 4x4s and a hotel minibus were sitting outside the doors, but otherwise the car park was empty. I had just turned around with a feeling of resignation, about to walk back into the building, when I spotted a car with its headlights on full and its hazard lights flashing, at the end of the long road to the airport. Squinting, I recognised Fardouza's rust-bucket, its window mechanism still broken. Safa was leaning out of the open window, her arms outstretched, shouting into the wind.

'Waris! Waris! Don't fly away without saying goodbye to me!'

Fardouza brought the car to a halt right in front of me. Safa wrenched the door open and rushed towards me.

'Mama, Mama, take me with you!'

I lifted the little one up and she wrapped her slender arms around me as tightly as she could.

'Will we really see each other again in Europe?' she sobbed loudly. 'Do you promise?'

I pressed her head gently to my shoulder with my right hand and stroked her hair. 'Safa, I always keep my promises. Have I ever disappointed you?'

The girl wiped away her tears and shook her head.

When I looked up, Fardouza was standing with Joanna, both of them wiping tears from their eyes. The African's car was still sitting in the road with its doors open, the engine running and the hazard lights on, right in front of the entrance to the terminal building.

I held Safa tightly, kissed her on the forehead and whispered: 'My little desert flower. We'll see each other again soon! Stay brave and strong until then.' While I was hugging Fardouza, Joanna cuddled the little one. Before the pain of leaving became too much, we turned and hurried towards border control.

I glanced back one last time and saw Safa, with her nose pressed against the large window that separated the customs area from the departures hall. She had placed her little hands flat on the pane. I raised my arm to wave to her a final time.

'Joanna,' I sighed, 'it's like you said: whoever saves a single human life saves the whole world.'

Saving Africa's little desert flowers was worth all the effort. Soon there would be thousands more. Safa would become an example for countless other girls; she was going to be my successor and continue my work. Maybe one day she would even achieve my goal, and end this terrible crime against innocent children once and for all.

A few minutes later we were taking off for Europe. As I looked out of the window, the sun was just climbing above the horizon. But it was already shining in my heart.

# 11

# Welcome to Paris

*Addis Ababa, 11 June 2013*

*Dear Waris,*

*I hope you are well. I miss you a lot and I was very sad when you had to go home after your lovely visit. But now I am super happy! Just a few more sleeps, then we'll see each other again.*

*I am still so pleased you invited us to Europe. We are sitting in the airport in Addis Ababa waiting for the plane to France. Papa says it's going to be a while before we can get on it. So I am writing you another letter, then the time will go faster.*

*The trip is very exciting. Maman, Amir and Nour cried a lot when we went through the big glass doors at the airport. There were men in uniforms everywhere and they waved a funny thing around us. And Inab's shoes beeped really loudly.*

*My friend Diane Pearl told me all about what happens*
*when you fly. She said I shouldn't be frightened at all. But*
*I wasn't frightened anyway. Papa is, though. When we*
*were in the long tube just before you get on, he wanted to*
*turn around and go home. Inab and I laughed. 'OK then,*
*we'll fly to Europe on our own,' we said. But then he got*
*on after all.*

*The cabin crew were very nice and they explained*
*everything to us. And they were funny too. Before we set*
*off they stood in front of us and showed us how to put on*
*a weird mask with air in it. 'But only in an emergency,'*
*the nice lady said. Then she waved her arms around, first*
*in front and behind, then in all directions. She looked*
*really silly.*

*Waris, I am sooo looking forward to seeing you again. I*
*have so much to tell you.*

*See you soon!*
*Je t'aime*
*Safa*

The letter that Safa had written to me just before her flight
to Paris only reached me at home in Danzig a week later,
where I was recovering from my latest exhausting trip. Over
the past few months Sophie, who worked in the Desert
Flower Foundation's Vienna office, had organised the
whole visit to Europe for Safa, her father and Inab. We were
taking them to Paris first; in France, they would at least
speak the language, which we hoped might lessen the culture shock. Later, they would travel to Austria and Germany.

In the meantime, Sophie had spoken to Idriss and Inab
on the phone several times, and prepared them as well as
she could for the first overseas trip of their lives. I had a

few personal things to take care of in Poland, and wanted to spend as much time as I could with my children over the summer holidays, so I would only be joining them in Germany. But I knew the three of them were in good hands with Sophie and my manager, Walter.

Eighteen-year-old Inab functioned as the tour leader for the little group. Safa was much too young, and Idriss was too fearful and disorganised, but for Inab the role of pack leader was not a new one.

## Sophie takes up the story

I had arrived from Vienna the previous evening, and together with Linda Weil-Curiel was waiting expectantly for the travellers from Djibouti. It was early morning in the arrivals hall, and dozens of passengers were streaming past us with loaded suitcases and bags, hugging their waiting relatives and disappearing through the exit.

Twenty minutes passed with no sign of the little group from Djibouti. The flow of travellers through the sliding doors slowed to a trickle, until finally the doors remained closed.

'Where can they be?' I was worried.

Linda was equally baffled. 'No idea. They can't still be in there, can they?' She let her gaze roam around the arrivals hall. 'Over there!' she suddenly cried.

She dashed over to a little dark-haired girl, took her by the shoulders and turned her round. The child stared at Linda in consternation as her parents pulled her away indignantly.

'I thought that was Safa. She looked so like her from a distance,' said Linda with a crestfallen expression as she walked back to where I was standing.

It was now just over an hour since the plane had landed.

'Maybe they wouldn't let them through the border when they changed planes in Frankfurt,' I mused. 'Or they could have missed their connecting flight in Addis Ababa, if they left the transit area and accidentally went through customs.'

'I just hope,' said Linda, voicing my own fears, 'that Idriss hasn't tried to bring khat to Europe with him and been arrested.'

I went to the information desk, but they couldn't tell me whether the three had been on board. I was about to start complaining when I heard Linda's joyful shout.

'There they are!'

Inab paused between the sliding doors, looking lost. Idriss was right behind her.

Safa pushed past them and bounded over to Linda, laughing.

'Keep moving!' an airport worker barked, ushering the two forcefully towards the exit.

Once everyone had been introduced, Idriss explained the delay. 'Our luggage is gone,' he said nervously.

Safa added with an air of disappointment: 'All of our clothes are in there ... and such a lovely present for you.'

'I'm sure your bags just got left behind when you changed planes,' I said. 'Go and sit down; I'll take care of it.'

Exhaustion was written on the faces of the arrivals from Djibouti. Inab and Idriss sank gratefully on to two plastic chairs in the arrivals hall, while I, holding Safa by the hand, went to look for the lost-luggage desk. A security officer went with us.

'Hello, little one. You were here just now, weren't you?' a friendly Frenchwoman said to Safa at the baggage reclaim.

I asked them to let me know as soon as the luggage was found, and handed the uniformed woman my business card.

'Oh, you work for the Desert Flower Foundation. Isn't that Waris Dirie's organisation?' she asked admiringly.

France has a very large African population, so the foundation is well known there. And even there, so far from their homeland, a lot of young women are affected by genital mutilation. As in all other European countries, gynaecologists carry out illegal circumcisions on women and little girls – for a huge fee, of course.

'Is that Waris Dirie's daughter?' the airline employee asked.

'No, she's sponsoring me,' Safa replied proudly in French. 'I played the little desert flower in her film.'

The woman at the counter couldn't hide her amazement.

In the meantime, Linda had organised a people-carrier taxi so that we could all travel into the city together.

'Wow, what a big car,' Inab marvelled.

Idriss, however, looked much less impressed, and used the burning stub of his cigarette to light another while I helped Safa into the car. When the little girl gripped the car door handle, the sleeve of her dress slid up, and I could see that her delicate, dark skin was covered in brown patterns that looked like tattoos.

'What are those?' I asked, spotting more patterns on Safa's legs.

'It's henna,' Inab explained.

Safa added: 'A friend of Maman's did them. You have to pay for them specially.'

On the way to the city centre, Inab explained the meaning of the signs, which she also had on her arms, to us Europeans. They were supposed to protect travellers from evil spirits.

As the taxi sped along the motorway towards the city centre, I asked to see our guests' passports.

Safa held hers out proudly. 'That's my first passport. Papa and I are the only ones in our family who have real ID now.'

I looked at the photo of Safa, and as I leafed through the document I discovered a folded piece of yellow paper. It was a letter, written in French by somebody with beautiful handwriting:

*Dear Waris Dirie*

*I acted in your film. In Djibouti I am a well-known actress and comedian. I heard from Fozia that you invited Inab and Safa to Europe.*

*Waris, please bring me and my three children to Europe too. I would like to become a famous actress and work in Hollywood. Please pay for our passports and visas and send us plane tickets.*

*Thank you*

*Roun*

There were two photos enclosed with the letter, and I recognised the woman who had played Waris's mother in *Desert Flower*. The pictures showed her and three children standing in front of a corrugated-iron shack. Without saying a word, I handed the letter to Linda, sitting behind me. She scanned it quickly and gave it back with a shake of her head.

'This is the problem,' she muttered. 'Everyone in Balbala thinks Waris can save them now.'

Inab, Idriss and Safa peered through the taxi's large windows, gaping at the buildings in the centre of Paris.

'Given that your luggage has gone missing, we should go and buy you some clothes,' I suggested. The girls' excitement at the shops they were passing had not escaped me. 'Or are you tired from the journey? Do you want to go and rest first?'

'No!' chorused Safa and Inab at once. 'We want to go to all these shops!'

But five minutes later, when I turned round again, Safa had fallen asleep. Inab and Idriss's eyes kept closing as well. I decided to put off the shopping trip and allow the guests to get some rest at the hotel first.

I called Waris in Poland as soon as they arrived in their rooms. I knew she'd have spent hours waiting impatiently for news from me. Her first question was of course about little Safa, whose arrival in Europe she had been looking forward to for weeks. I told her everything that had happened so far, and outlined our plans for the coming week.

'I'll be with you as soon as I can,' Waris promised.

'I have to hang up now, somebody's knocking on my door,' I replied, adding: 'I'll call you right back.'

When I opened the door, Idriss was standing outside, looking tired and anxious. With a lighter in his hand, he gesticulated wildly, saying: 'Cigarettes! Cigarettes!' His strong accent made the words sound like a hostile bark. I am also a smoker, so I fetched a packet from my suitcase and handed it to Idriss, but he just looked at the gift with a sullen expression.

'Two!' he said imperiously.

*Why is this guy being so unfriendly?* I wondered. But in spite of my annoyance, I didn't want to get into a debate with him, so I brought him a second packet and closed the door without saying goodbye.

On the phone with Waris again, I told her what had happened.

'You know, Sophie,' she explained, 'this man has never been abroad in his life, and he doesn't know you. He's just feeling insecure.'

'There's still no reason to behave like that.'

'You need to keep an eye on him,' Waris told me, concerned that the situation could get out of hand. 'Like most men in Djibouti, Idriss chews a lot of khat, and I'm sure he must be addicted to it. Don't let him out of your sight, or he could get up to more mischief.'

My heart sank but I promised to look after him.

After hanging up, I walked over to the window and looked down at the street outside the hotel, which was sparkling in the sunlight. *I hope we haven't made a mistake, and the culture shock isn't too much for the three of them.* I knew the trip had to be a success – otherwise the plan to save Safa was in danger.

In the late afternoon, once I had got some rest as well, I decided to check on my charges. I spent several minutes knocking on the door to Inab and Safa's room. After what seemed like an age, a tousled Inab opened the door. She pointed to the bed, where Safa was fast asleep, barely visible under the covers.

I sat down on the edge of the bed, stroked Safa's hair and whispered: 'Well then, little one, are you hungry?'

The girl slowly opened her eyes, stretched contentedly and nodded.

Idriss was just as difficult to wake, and when he finally opened the door to his room, I was greeted by a cloud of thick smoke.

'You're not allowed to smoke in the hotel rooms,' I explained to him firmly.

Unimpressed, Safa's father put his trousers on and followed me down to the hotel lobby, where the two of us waited for Inab and Safa. Thick carpets, velvet-covered armchairs and small tables made of dark wood gave the hotel a typically elegant, French feel. Once Idriss had had a look around, he got his cigarettes and lighter out of his trouser pocket and calmly lit up.

'You can't smoke here!' The concierge had hurried out from behind his desk before I even had a chance to react.

But the Somali made no move to put the cigarette out. He just stood there, puffing away in front of the concierge.

'*Monsieur*, please put that cigarette out at once,' the latter urged him once again.

No chance. On the spur of the moment, I took the butt from Idriss's mouth and went out into the street to get rid of it. I then apologised to the concierge and tried to explain to him that smoking was allowed everywhere in Djibouti, and it was my guest's first time in Europe.

At that moment, Safa and Inab got out of the lift, laughing. 'Sophie, there's a flying room here, just like in the hotel where I stayed with Waris in Djibouti,' Safa said excitedly, even managing to coax a smile out of the furious concierge.

The situation was saved for the time being, and we strolled through the streets of Paris in search of a restaurant. Inab, Safa and the permanently smoking Idriss stared wide-eyed at their surroundings. They were just starting to realise how far they had come from their homeland, and grasp the contrast with the terrible conditions there.

'Paris Orléans Viande d'Aubrac,' Safa read solemnly from the red awning of a little brasserie that I was steering them towards. 'Sounds great!'

As the sun was shining – and as it meant that Idriss could feed his nicotine habit in peace – we settled on a table outside.

Safa wanted chicken and chips and a Coke; Inab ordered Coke as well, and the fish; and I chose a steak and salad. Idriss just ordered a Coke.

'Would you like something to eat as well, Monsieur?' the waiter asked politely.

Safa's father pointed a finger at one of the dishes on the menu.

'Are you sure about that?' the waiter enquired, a note of irritation in his voice.

'*Oui, oui,*' Idriss snapped, rudely waving him away.

When the food was served fifteen minutes later, a plate was set down in front of everyone except Idriss.

'Where's my food? I'm hungry!' barked Idriss.

'*Monsieur,*' the waiter replied, 'don't you want to wait?'

But Safa's father insisted that his food was served right away. The waiter left the table shaking his head.

'What did you order?' I asked, thinking that I should have asked him this much earlier.

'Fish,' he said curtly.

A few minutes later the waiter returned with a bowl in his hand. '*Voilà*, monsieur ... your fruit salad.'

'I didn't order that,' Idriss snarled at the man, whose patience was wearing thin.

The waiter flicked open the menu and pointed at the line Idriss had indicated when he ordered.

The man's eyes glittered with anger and shame. His face was burning.

But rather than apologise, he insisted: 'I wanted fish.'

The waiter served the fruit salad without another word. I noticed that we all kept our eyes on our plates, in an effort not to embarrass Idriss any further. Safa's lip-smacking was the only thing that broke the awkward silence. Unfazed by the situation, she was contentedly demolishing her chicken, and pushing one *frite* after another into her little mouth. Her father meanwhile started jiggling his legs under the table, making it wobble. Suddenly he snatched Safa's plate from under her nose and started eating her chicken and chips.

Safa had remained unruffled by the fact that her father couldn't read, and had argued loudly with the waiter in front of everyone. But when it came to food, she wasn't going to stand for any nonsense. 'Hey!' she cried, glaring at him like a little lioness.

When Idriss ignored her complaint, the girl looked over at me in desperation.

'Idriss, leave the little one her food. I'm sure your fish is on its way now,' I said, trying to make him see sense.

'No, no,' he replied with his mouth full. 'It's fine ...'

A few moments later, Safa's plate was empty.

Still, in the end everyone had enough to eat: I ordered another two large portions of chips, and then desserts.

After dinner they all leaned back in their chairs, relaxed and weary. While we waited for the bill, Safa's father lit one cigarette after another.

'We're tired, call us a taxi,' he said, turning to me. 'I don't like to walk any more.'

On our way to the taxi rank, we passed one of Paris's many brightly coloured fruit stalls. 'Can we buy something?' Safa asked, filled with curiosity.

I took the two girls up to the colourfully decorated stall. 'What would you like then?'

Inab and Safa looked helplessly at the fresh fruit heaped in front of them.

'What are those?' Safa pointed at the blackberries. 'And those?' She had never seen strawberries before either.

'Those are grapes,' Inab said, clearly proud that she knew the name of the fruit. She took the grapes in both hands and held them up with a big smile.

The stallholder was less impressed with the girl's knowledge, instructing me to tell them not to go touching everything.

'You know, Sophie,' Inab explained, while I got my money out, 'my name means grape. My parents called me that because when I was little, I was as sweet as a grape.' Inab looked awkwardly at the ground. As soon as she had spoken the words, she must have thought of her mother. Her eyes began to shine.

I gave the girl a hug, and said to the stallholder: 'We'll take two bags of those lovely sweet grapes.'

'My parents called me Sophie, which means "wisdom". What does your name mean?' I said, turning to Safa, who was engrossed in the glittering window of the boutique next door.

Sophie with Inab and Safa in Europe.

Idriss's gaze was fixed on the concrete under his feet. He answered for her. 'Safa is a holy name,' he said without looking up. 'In Mecca there are two holy mountains: Safa and Marwah. When my daughter was born we gave her both names, but even as a baby we just called her Safa.'

The guests' tiredness seemed to have faded away, and when they were sitting in the taxi shortly afterwards, the girls couldn't stop staring.

'Wow!' said Safa as we passed the Eiffel Tower.

The taxi driver was delighted with his passengers' interest, and told her what it was. Clearly an enterprising man, he did an impromptu lap of honour and took a little detour along the Champs-Elysées.

'I've never seen such a big house,' Inab marvelled.

Safa asked how many people lived in the Eiffel Tower.

The taxi driver, astonished at the ignorance of tourists today, threw me a quizzical glance.

'It's not a house, it's the emblem of Paris,' I told the two girls. 'But you can visit the tower and go up it in a flying room.'

Safa stared in disbelief at the steel construction stretching up into the sky in front of her. 'Why did the French people build such a big house if nobody can live there?' she asked indignantly. 'I don't understand.'

The taxi driver couldn't suppress his curiosity any longer. 'I've never heard anything like it,' he smiled, talking to me as if I was the only person in the car. 'Where do they come from?'

'*They* are from Djibouti,' I retorted. 'Do you know where that is?' I was annoyed by the disdainful comment from the driver.

He answered hesitantly: 'Yes, of course: it's somewhere in India.'

# 12

# A shopping trip

I was woken the following morning by the sound of my mobile ringing. Groaning with tiredness, I looked at the time: just after six.

'Hello?' I muttered.

'Good-morning *madame*,' trilled the cheerful woman at the other end of the line. 'We've found your luggage. It was left in Addis Ababa, and it will be here in forty-eight hours at the most.'

At least the day had begun with some good news, I thought, before dragging herself to the bathroom, where I allowed myself a lot longer than usual to get ready. Eventually, I dialled the extension for Idriss's room. When he didn't pick up, I went down to the floor below and knocked on his door. There was no reaction there, either. I was starting to worry – I remembered Waris's warning, and the butterflies in my stomach were not a good sign. Where was Idriss? Was he still fast asleep, despite going to bed so early the night before? Or had he gone out?

I knocked again. Nothing.

Having searched the breakfast room in vain, scanned the lobby and asked about him at reception, I ran out into the street. Was it possible he had taken heed of the French laws and was smoking outside? But there was no trace of Safa's father there, either. Where could he be? My heart was pounding. Idriss didn't know his way around Paris. Maybe he had gone out for cigarettes and got lost. I didn't bother calling his mobile – shortly after their arrival, they had discovered he couldn't get a signal in Europe; his African provider obviously didn't have a roaming agreement with France.

Defeated, I went back to the breakfast room. It was pointless wandering around the huge city trying to find him.

I had just ordered a coffee when Idriss came in. Without greeting me, he went straight to the buffet, loaded a plate with cheese, jam and toast, and took a seat at my table.

'Where have you been?' I asked. 'I've been looking for you everywhere.'

'I just went for a little walk round the block,' he replied with his mouth full. He took a slurp of my coffee when the waitress brought it to the table. But the smell of freshly brewed coffee couldn't disguise the alcohol fumes that escaped from his mouth.

'Are you drunk?' I asked.

'Nonsense! I just went to buy cigarettes!' Idriss cried indignantly.

The previous evening, I had given him twenty euros for emergencies. A mistake, as it turned out.

'I was worried,' I told him. 'Please don't just go off

without letting me know. I'm responsible for you all. Waris would never forgive me if anything happened to you.'

'Where is Waris, anyway? There is an urgent matter I need to discuss with her,' Idriss asked, ignoring my concern. Without waiting for an answer, he got up and went to get more food from the buffet.

When he came back, I said: 'I spoke to Waris on the phone yesterday; she's going to come and meet us soon.' *Hopefully*, I added silently to myself.

Then I went to wake Safa and Inab, so they could have breakfast together. The girls enjoyed their food, and we all set out for the city centre, to go shopping as promised. Our first challenge was getting through the ticket barriers at the Metro station.

'You put the ticket in here, and then you just walk through,' I said, demonstrating for the group.

Anxiously Safa put a hand on the metal bars that were blocking the way just below her chin.

'No, I don't want to go through there,' she said.

'Go on, don't make such a fuss. Just walk through!' Idriss snapped at his daughter. 'It can't be that hard.'

Safa was still looking intimidated, and she didn't move until Inab took her hand and gently led her through the barrier. Next it was Idriss's turn. Without a moment's hesitation, he put his underground ticket in the slot – of the wrong machine. When he pushed against the barrier right in front of him, it didn't budge an inch.

'This thing is broken!' he shouted.

'The machine you put your ticket in is for the next barrier along,' I explained, trying to be patient. 'You have to go through there.'

Instead of moving across, Idriss simply vaulted over the

metal bar. 'That's how we solve problems at home,' he said drily, showing his brown-stained teeth. For the first time since his arrival in Paris, he gave a hearty laugh.

Having reached the department store without further mishaps, I relaxed. I was looking forward to styling the two girls, who had been forced to get back into their crumpled, sweaty clothes from the day before.

'What's your favourite colour?' I asked little Safa while we were still on the ground floor.

Young Parisians and tourists were already rummaging through the shelves and rails of brightly coloured clothes. Inab and Safa looked around excitedly, as if they had suddenly found themselves in Shangri-La.

'Orange, yellow, pink. And yours?' replied Safa, unable to tear her gaze away from all the clothes.

'What a coincidence, those are my favourite colours too!' I carried on walking through the aisles. 'And I like turquoise and purple too. Do you?' When Safa didn't answer, I turned to look for her. She hadn't followed me; she was staring open-mouthed at a woman who was heading to the till carrying about twenty pieces of clothing.

'You must have a very big family,' Safa said innocently to the woman.

She just shook her head in bewilderment.

'Come on, Safa. We're going to find some things for you. But we'll have to go to the children's department,' I said, not guessing that the next hurdle was just around the corner.

In front of the escalator, my three companions stopped as if rooted to the ground.

'Help, the stairs are moving!' This time it was Inab who had taken fright. Safa and Idriss didn't trust the moving staircase either. I had my work cut out to convince the three of them to go up to the first floor. When I described the incident to Waris later over the phone, she laughed. 'The first time I saw an escalator,' she said, 'shortly after my arrival in London, I was just as sceptical. There is so much about Safa and her story that reminds me of mine.'

When I saw Inab and Safa staring in astonishment at all the dresses, T-shirts, trousers, skirts, socks and shoes, I was conscious once again of how lucky European children were. Idriss meanwhile was just staring into space, looking bored.

'I'm going to go out for a minute and smoke,' he said.

After he had promised me that he would come straight back, I could do nothing but let him go.

'Right, Safa, which of these things do you like best?' I went to one of the many children's concessions and started picking up clothes and presenting them to her, realising that I sounded like an enthusiastic saleswoman in a designer boutique. 'This skirt here? Or this pinky-red one? Do you like denim?'

'I don't really need anything,' the girl said quietly. But then she pointed a timid finger at the denim skirt, and a grin spread across her little face.

Half an hour later we had chosen a few items, and went looking for a changing room, into which Safa disappeared by herself.

After a few minutes the little girl called me frantically. I pushed the curtain aside to see that Safa's head was stuck in a T-shirt that she was struggling to put on over the top of her clothes. 'It's much too small,' she groaned.

After I had freed Safa, I explained that you had to strip

to your underwear in order to try things on. It was ignorance, not clumsiness that had got Safa into this situation: the girl had never picked clothes out herself before. All her life she had worn other people's cast-offs. She eventually decided on a pair of Hello Kitty trainers, since her sandals were threatening to fall apart – as well as the skirt, two T-shirts, a hairband and a summer dress.

'These are great!' Safa cried, spotting a pair of pink sunglasses. She put them on the wrong way up, so that they slipped lopsided over her eyes.

It made me laugh. 'Wait a minute,' I said, carefully removing the sunglasses from Safa's face. 'Do you see the indentation here? That's for your nose.' Then I turned Safa's new favourite thing the other way up and set it back on the girl's button nose.

Safa admired herself from every angle in one of the giant mirrors.

It was Inab's turn next, so we went down to the young women's department on the escalator, which the girls still eyed suspiciously. Idriss had not yet returned from his cigarette break, but I assumed that he was looking round the men's department.

Inab might have been shy when we first entered the shop, but she now went into a buying frenzy. The pile of clothes in her arms grew from one minute to the next. Underwear, clothes, shoes, make-up – no clothes rail or table was safe from the eighteen-year-old. 'I want this!' she cried excitedly. 'And that too.'

'Inab, I'm afraid I can't buy you that many things,' I said, trying to slow her down. 'We have to save some money to get Idriss kitted out.'

Disappointed, Inab paused for a second to put back a

few of the things she had draped over her outstretched arm.

When Inab opened the curtain of the changing room a short while later, I couldn't help but think of the movies. Instead of the shy African girl in a long brown skirt, a holey grey vest and an old-fashioned shawl, here was an attractive young woman in yellow jeans, a bright white shirt and stylish summer boots. The ugly duckling had become a beautiful swan: a young lady whom you could have taken to a business meeting without a second thought.

'Will I pass as a new employee of the Desert Flower Foundation?' Inab asked, laughing. Her posture showed that the new look had also given her a new self-confidence.

'You could even pass as a model!' I replied happily.

'Well, then I'll need a few other outfits ... maybe this leather jacket as well?' Inab ventured.

But that made me impatient and I told the girl to get back into the changing room, a little more sternly than before. Inab changed back into her own clothes and plodded sulkily along behind us as we headed to the men's department to look for Idriss. In fact, Safa's father had already picked out some clothes and was waiting for the three of us.

'Good work, Idriss,' I said, feeling relieved – though when I saw the winter coat he was holding, I added: 'You probably don't need that here. It's the start of summer, and it's getting warmer every day. That coat is much too warm for Djibouti as well.'

Idriss just snatched the coat back out of my hands and glowered at me furiously.

Inab burst out laughing. 'We get quite cold in the mornings and evenings here,' she explained to me, much to my surprise. 'In Djibouti the temperature never goes below thirty, even at night.'

'OK, then we'll buy the padded jacket to stop you freezing,' I laughed.

But I wasn't laughing a few minutes later, when Idriss and I were standing together in the queue for the tills.

He leaned over and whispered in my ear: 'I need the jacket for the winter in Europe. We're going to stay here.'

A shudder ran down my spine. What did he mean by that? And how did he imagine it was going to happen? It was time to have a serious word with Safa's father.

An opportunity for this didn't arise until after dinner.

After we'd been shopping, we had taken a tour of the city, and then gone back to the hotel to recover. Then we headed out again and, at Safa's request, ordered burgers, chips and Coke at McDonald's. Back in the hotel, the girls rushed off to their rooms at once. They had discovered MTV, and danced wildly around their room to the beats of European chart hits they had never heard before, until collapsing into bed exhausted and falling asleep.

When I had closed the door to the girls' room behind me, I turned to Idriss. 'Come on, let's go out and sit in the garden for a while. We can drink and smoke out there,' I said, to lure the chain smoker outside.

Idriss agreed, though he clearly wasn't interested in having a conversation.

Several minutes passed in silence, while I searched for the right words.

'Are you finding it hard that your wife stayed behind on her own, with the two boys?' I ventured cautiously.

Safa's father took a sip of the beer the waiter had just

brought him. His new clothes, including the bright orange padded jacket he had on in spite of the twenty-degree temperature outside, made him look a lot younger than the worn-out things he had been wearing when he arrived in Paris. He lit a cigarette, and in the glow of the lighter I could see that his expression had changed. Fear and anger had turned into a deep longing.

'I can hardly sleep, because I am so worried,' he said. Thick smoke billowed out between his brown teeth. 'I have never been apart from *ma chérie* before. Luckily she is with relatives in Addis Ababa, and not alone in Djibouti.' Then he fell silent again.

I waited for him to carry on.

'My sons Mohammed and Nour are with their grandparents. They are the most important thing in the world to me. I miss them very much.'

Confused, I asked: 'Safa always talks about *Amir* and Nour. Have I missed something?'

Idriss grinned. He seemed to enjoy talking about his family. 'Do you have a piece of paper?' he asked.

Then he reached into his coat pocket and took out a pen from his hotel room. I rummaged in my handbag, found a grubby scrap of paper and handed it to him. Writing like a small child, he scrawled a few wobbly, barely legible letters on it.

'Idriss Nour Souldan,' he read out very slowly. 'That is my full name. Where we come from, children have their father's first two names as well as their given names.' He scribbled again. 'So my daughter is Safa Idriss Nour. And my five-year-old is Mohammed Amir Idriss Nour.'

'So why do you call him Amir, when his first name is Mohammed?'

The father of three proudly explained: 'As a good
Muslim, you cannot give a child the name Mohammed
without another name. And so at home we call him Amir,
but when he goes to school he will be Mohammed.'

I looked hard at the piece of paper and asked: 'So your
youngest is Nour Idriss Nour, right?'

Idriss nodded. 'Exactly. He's three years old now. My
sons are good boys.'

While he took another gulp of his beer, I probed a little
further. 'Waris told me that your older son has some
health problems. Can I ask what's wrong with him?'

Idriss's countenance darkened at once. 'My son has had
a serious lung sickness ever since he was small. He had
coughing that got worse from day to day. Then he just lay
in bed wheezing. I thought he would die. Never in my life
did I cry before then, but then I did.' With downcast eyes,
he told me that Amir was a strong boy, and had spent
months fighting for his life. 'A woman we know in Balbala
is a healer. Although we had hardly anything to give her,
we called her again and again. But even she could do nothing. At night we hardly slept, because we had to carry
Mohammed around, so he didn't suffocate lying down.'

It was only when Safa appeared in *Desert Flower* and he
signed the contract with the Desert Flower Foundation
that they were able to do something for his son.

'That's how we got medicines and we got to see Dr
Acina, who treats Mohammed regularly. Even so, he probably won't grow to be very old,' Idriss added, turning away
to hide the tears in his eyes.

I instantly regretted pressing him. This man was
carrying a heavy burden on his shoulders. His concern
for the son he had left behind to travel to Europe must

be what was driving Idriss out of bed so early in the morning – and probably fuelling his alcohol consumption.

'I am very proud of my sons,' Idriss repeated.

'You can be very proud of Safa as well. She really is a wonderful, smart little girl,' I told him.

Idriss shrugged silently. He didn't seem to enjoy talking about his daughter as much as he had enjoyed telling me about her brothers. That might have been because girls didn't count for much in his society. But maybe it was also because, since Safa was still intact, she put the family in a position that was not always pleasant.

It made me worry. If Safa's mother want to have her circumcised one day, in spite of the contract with the foundation, was that Idriss's secret wish as well?

Before Safa's arrival in Europe, Waris had spoken to me about her clash with Fozia after the fashion show. She had told me about Fozia's parting remark, and that she was afraid the old woman would make sure the girl was eventually circumcised.

I decided to use this opportunity to find out about Fatouma, Idriss's mother, to see if Waris's suspicion that she was a cutter was true.

'My father died when I was a child,' Idriss told me. 'My mother had to bring up my brothers and sisters and me by herself.'

I expressed admiration. I imagined that would be a difficult task. 'My mother is a very strong, special woman,' Idriss went on with pride in his voice. 'She looked after us well, and always earned her own money. Although we had no father, we were a very respected family.'

A respected woman in the Balbala slums? A woman who earned her own money? I was almost certain that Fatouma had supported her family with the horrific mutilation of little girls. The thought gave me goose-bumps. It meant Safa was in great danger.

'Let's go back inside. I'm tired,' I said, steering the conversation away from this sensitive subject. I knew it was pointless talking to Idriss about his mother's occupation when he so clearly looked up to her, so I said good-night.

On the way back to my room, I dialled Waris's number in Poland and told her I was worried about Idriss, with his mysterious vanishing acts, his early-morning drinking and his surly manner. Waris listened without comment as I described what we had done that day, and what I had discovered.

'Waris, I'm at a loss,' I finally said. 'On the one hand, this man desperately needs our support to save his son from suffocating, and on the other, I'm sure his mother is just waiting to mutilate Safa. Even if right now Idriss is saying he'll never have his daughter cut, one day he might just give in to the pressure from this woman.

'Maybe we should grant his wish and bring the whole family to Europe. Maybe that's why he wants to be here, to save his sick son and his daughter,' I went on, without pausing for breath.

'Sophie, you know that's completely unrealistic. It can't be the solution,' said Waris. 'Even if we could bring this one African family over here, we'd be abandoning the hundreds of thousands who would remain behind. And bringing people from Africa to Europe isn't a cure-all, either,' she explained. 'We have to think of another plan – a plan that Safa can have some real involvement in. I've been doing some thinking about it over the last few days, but I'd prefer to discuss it with you when I get there.

'Don't worry too much,' she tried to reassure me. 'Enjoy the rest of your time in Paris. At least Safa is safe here in Europe.'

It was important to Waris that Safa and Inab enjoyed the trip, and had as many new experiences as possible: experiences of a world where women played an equal role fit for human beings. Experiences that would soon be of use to them back in their homeland.

# 13

# Inab's story

*Paris, 14 July 2013*

*Dear Waris*

  *It's a shame you are still not here. But I hope you are having a nice holiday with your children. Sophie said I can always write to you. She will send you my letter on the computer. Inab says you can read the letter straight away then, and you won't have to wait for the post. In Europe you have a lot of great things that we don't have in Djibouti.*

  *Here almost everything is great. I am very, very happy to be here. Inab is my friend now, she likes Europe too. Sophie is also very nice to us and she bought us a lot of lovely things already. I got a denim skirt. I'll show it to you soon, when we see each other!*

  *Today there was a big party in Paris. Sophie said it was because of the national day. All the streets were full of*

*people. I don't think there are that many people in the
whole of Djibouti. Then some planes painted coloured
stripes on the sky. Sophie said they were the colours of the
French flag. I've never seen anything like that. There were
a whole lot of tanks driving down the lovely street with the
big white gate at the end, and soldiers marching with
guns. And there were policemen everywhere. Then I was a
bit scared. When we're at home in Djibouti, Papa always
tells us to stay away from soldiers and policemen. Sophie
says the police are there for our protection. I don't know if
that's true, so I hid from them just in case.*

*When we were in the hotel before, Papa came to see me
and Inab in our room. He has a plan. He wants to stay in
Europe with us. Now he wants to find some important
people to ask if we can stay here.*

*I don't really know if I want to do that. I miss Maman
and Nour and Amir. And my best friend Diane Pearl. I
will never be a Frenchwoman – I will always be an Issa.
Papa says the Issa tribe is the best in the whole of Africa.
And that Maman is sometimes a bit funny because she is
a Darod. Like you, Waris. Papa says the Darods are crazy.
But you're not crazy at all. In Djibouti only an Issa is
allowed to be President. When I grow up I want to be
President of Djibouti. Or a paediatrician. Or both.
Whatever happens I want to help the children in Djibouti.
And you have to tell me how to do that, Waris.*

*I am really looking forward to seeing you.*

*Kisses*

*Safa*

Although it was already after midnight, I sat down at the
little desk in my hotel room, opened my email and typed

out the words Safa had set down in her wobbly hand-writing. At the passage *He wants to stay in Europe with us. Now he wants to find some important people to ask if we can stay here,* I faltered. A few things that had happened over the last few days suddenly made sense. It was Bastille Day, and I had been going to show our guests the Eiffel Tower when Idriss had vanished again. Then he reappeared out of nowhere, in a foul mood. Suddenly I said out loud to myself, 'He went looking for the Djibouti Embassy. That's it.'

I hurriedly changed the subject line of my email to Waris:

**Letter from Safa. Warning: Idriss is looking for the embassy.**

That night I didn't sleep well, worried that Idriss might be about to abscond. Still, I tried to give nothing away the following morning, and made an effort to give Inab and Safa as many experiences as I could of life far from their homeland. There was a visit to the fair planned for that day. Idriss immediately said he wanted to stay in the hotel by himself, but that rang all kinds of alarm bells. Under no circumstances was I going to leave him alone for a whole morning.

The two girls' beaming smiles soon almost made me forget my worries. Safa's and Inab's eyes shone with happiness as they pushed their way through the narrow aisles, past dozens of stalls and snack stands, towards the flashing carousel. I was pleased that the two were in such high spirits; over the past few days they had really loosened up. And the carousel was just the beginning: chair swings, bumper cars, tin can alley, candyfloss, clowns – they were wildly excited, trying everything and letting themselves be spun through the air without any fear. At the bumper cars, Safa found herself a little red Porsche and drove around in it with a girl who had big, blonde curls, her chest swelling with pride. The French girl eyed her dark-skinned driving partner shyly as Safa tried and failed to get the car under control.

'Right! Left! Not over there!' Proud that his daughter was showing an interest in driving – something that, in his country, was the sole preserve of men – Idriss gave her tips from the sidelines.

When I tried to take a photo of the two little drivers at the end, the blonde girl hid her face behind Safa's back with a look of anxiety. It was only when Safa gave her a big hug that she too let out a joyful laugh.

This sensitive, open-minded little girl made friends quickly wherever she was in the world.

That afternoon, tired and completely overwhelmed by all these new impressions, we took the overcrowded Metro back to the hotel. Inab, who had been so carefree and joyful at the fair, suddenly went very quiet, and kept grimacing as if she was in real pain.

'What's wrong?' I asked. 'Does it hurt?'

'Yes,' groaned Inab. 'But I'm used to it. I have it every month.'

I took her into the nearest chemist's. I asked Idriss to wait outside with Safa, and ushered Inab into the shop, to the shelf of feminine-hygiene products. She stood and looked at them, wide-eyed and perplexed.

'So, if I were you, I'd get these,' I said, picking up a packet of sanitary towels and holding it out to the girl.

'What are those?'

Once again I was brought up short, realising that Inab had grown up in a completely different world – a world where it seemed that nobody was interested in how a woman dealt with her period. A world where it was completely normal for a woman who had undergone genital mutilation to suffer terrible pain once a month, far worse than the cramps other women experienced.

Fortunately, once we had been to the pharmacy for a fast-acting painkiller, Inab soon started to feel better. The medicine released her from her pain for a few hours at least, and over dinner in a pizzeria she was visibly more relaxed. The four of us had ice-cream, then wandered past a little flea market where people from all over the world were selling their goods.

'We have a market like this in the old town of Djibouti,' Idriss explained. The colourful cloths, the exotic smell of spices and incense from far-off lands and the traders, many of whom were African, were clearly making him homesick.

He suggested going for a proper look around the flea market, but only Safa was keen on the idea. So we split up, and while father and daughter plunged into the crowds, Inab and I took a rest.

We sat down on a concrete bench at the edge of the marketplace, where an old accordion player was playing *chansons*. For a while we listened in silence to the music's melancholy tones. 'My mother plays an instrument too,' Inab said suddenly. 'When I was little, she often used to play to me on her wooden flute. It was lovely.' Her eyes began to shine.

'Your mother went away?'

'Maman is sick,' Inab explained, with a tremor in her voice. 'So a few years ago she went to Ethiopia, to her family, so they would take care of her and she could get better. At first we thought she wouldn't be away for long, but then the years went by and she didn't come back.' The young woman stared thoughtfully into her empty ice-cream tub, in which only the small green plastic spoon remained. 'Then, four weeks ago, she suddenly turned up at our door.'

Surprised by this news, I leaned forward. 'Really? That's incredible!'

'Yes, we could hardly believe it. She was away for more than five years,' said Inab, tears starting to run down her cheeks. 'You can't imagine how happy I am that she is finally back. Now we're a proper family again. And I don't have to worry about my sisters while I'm here. You know, Sophie, I would do anything for my sisters.'

I told her I understood: I too come from a big family. 'Tell me about your little sisters,' I said, putting an arm around Inab's shoulders.

'They're called Hibo and Hamda. Hamda is the older one: she was born in 2002 and she's already at school,' Inab explained. 'Hibo is four years younger and she is going to start school after the holidays.' So the girls were eleven and seven. 'Yes, I think that's right,' Inab said uncertainly.

Over the last few days, I had often noticed that when Idriss and Safa talked about their siblings, parents or friends, they could never say exactly how old they were. They seemed to estimate even their own ages.

The accordion player waved his hat under our noses with a plea for a small donation, and I threw a few coins into it. Then I lowered my voice: 'Can I ask you another personal question?' I was worried about her two sisters.

Inab gave me a suspicious look, but finally agreed with a little nod of her head.

'Is it true that your sisters haven't been circumcised yet?'

'Yes,' the girl replied. 'I fought tooth and nail so they would not have to go through this torture as well.' She held her right hand to her lower abdomen, which had obviously started to hurt again. 'But I did it. So far, they have been spared. You know,' said Inab, playing with the spoon in her ice-cream tub, 'I fought against being circumcised for years as well. I was always coming up with new excuses so they would leave me alone. I told my parents they would have to put it off, because at my age there could be big complications. I even said I'd heard that at a certain age parts of the vagina could grow back. So I managed to avoid it for a long time. Until four years ago.'

Inab turned to me.

'I really hoped they would just forget about it. But then they did it anyway. I was terribly afraid of the pain, and I fought against it so much that they chose the least severe form of circumcision for me.'

I realised that meant they had cut away her clitoris.

I had heard so many stories of women who had experienced this gruesome ritual, but each one still shocked me. I felt hugely impressed by this girl's strength.

'I think it's wonderful that you're protecting your little sisters,' I said.

Inab looked at me intently. 'In Djibouti, Waris said she wants to help me make this horrible pain stop. Do you know anything about that?'

I assumed that what Waris had in mind was an operation to reverse the damage. Within the foundation, we were all agreed that our aim should not only be to prevent the genital mutilation of young girls, but also to help those who were already suffering the terrible consequences of this torture. Over the last year, the Desert Flower Foundation had scoured the globe for doctors who could give mutilated women a new, pain-free life – and the chance of something approaching normal sexuality.

I was about to tell Inab a bit about this when Idriss returned, holding his daughter by the hand. Inab was visibly disappointed: she was only too keen to know how – and above all when – we could help her.

'Let's have a proper talk about this some other time,' I promised.

'We bought such lovely things,' said Safa, proudly showing Inab and me a well-thumbed comic book. 'Papa found a cigarette case!'

Idriss pulled a decorated metal box out of his trouser pocket, opened it and immediately took out a cigarette.

'Oh, but he's going to spend all his time refilling it!' I laughed.

In the hotel, our exhausted group was greeted with some good news.

'Your missing luggage has arrived,' said the young lady on reception, pointing at two bags whose shabby condition betrayed their owners' poverty. Beaming, Idriss, Inab and Safa picked up their meagre luggage and dragged it to the lift.

'You have to come with us.' Safa pulled me into her room, dropped the bag and rushed to open it. 'This is a cake from Djibouti.' She proudly held out a squashed cake in a woven basket. 'It's for you. And for Waris. And for the people in the office in Vienna. And for everyone.'

I was touched by the little girl's eagerness to give everyone a present. It showed how grateful she was for this trip. 'That's so thoughtful of you. We'll all eat it together when we meet Waris.'

'When *are* we going to meet Waris?' asked Inab, who had sat down on the floor with us.

'You know what?' I was keen to do something nice for the girls in return. 'Let's give her a quick call.' Inab and Safa leapt around the room whooping. 'You'll have to be a bit quieter,' I said, putting my finger to my lips, 'otherwise I won't hear when she picks up.

'Hello, Waris? There are two young ladies sitting next to me who would very much like to speak to you.'

Safa warbled happily into the receiver: 'Hello, Waris. It's me, the little desert flower.'

Without pausing for breath, she spent several minutes telling Waris about her stay in Paris, and all the things she had seen – and of course, about the cake.

'Oh, thank you! I'm really looking forward to it,' Waris said. 'You're going to Vienna next, with Sophie, and you'll see our office. And after that we'll see each other again, and have a lovely time together.'

Safa was clearly overjoyed. After saying goodbye with a loud kiss, she handed the phone to her older friend.

'Hello, Inab, how are you?' Waris asked the eighteen-year-old.

'Not so good today,' she answered honestly. 'I'm having pains.'

'Inab, you know we will help you if you want us to,' was all Waris said.

Whether the young woman would want to undergo surgery after everything that had been done to her in the past, however, was another matter. Waris didn't want to discuss such a sensitive issue over the phone, so she just said, 'Let's talk about it when we meet in Germany.'

'We'll see,' Inab said sceptically. She must have been finding it difficult to believe there was actually a solution for her problem. She said a brief '*Ciao*' and passed Waris back to me.

I knew that Waris was having the same thought: *I hope we're not going to fall short of Inab's expectations.*

# 14

# Concerns for Safa

Our unconventional little tour party's stay in Paris was drawing to a close. Idriss had changed: there were no more sudden disappearances; he chatted amicably with me and the girls, and showed an interest in the city and its sights. Admittedly, he was still smoking like a chimney and never missed an opportunity to have a drink, but overall he seemed much more open and friendly. I had no idea what lay behind this transformation, but I decided to place a little more faith in him, and granted him a morning with no children or sightseeing. He stayed behind in the hotel while I took the girls shopping again.

Inab and Safa had changed as well. Initially tense and uncertain, they were now moving through the streets of Paris like little Europeans. Our plan to gradually acclimatise the three visitors to European life had worked. Escalators, barriers and underground trains were no longer obstacles. *How quickly people adapt to changing circumstances, whether for better or worse,* I thought as the three of us walked into a department store. Just as before, Inab was scarcely able to control herself and wanted everything she saw, and Safa was once again more than modest. She had no idea why they were going shopping again – after all, their luggage had arrived now.

The girls were allowed to put on their new things right away, and when Safa opened the changing-room curtain wearing a frilly white dress, I was speechless. The white material emphasised the little girl's delicate, dark skin, and above the neckline I could see the hand-of-Fatima pendant that Waris had given her. On the spur of the moment, I grabbed my smartphone and took a photo.

But to my horror, when I zoomed in on the picture I saw a mark under Safa's eye. I examined the girl's face, running my fingers gently over the dark patch, which looked even worse close up than it had on the photo.

'Ow!' squealed Safa.

'What *is* that?' I asked.

Safa turned away. 'I don't know. I've got one on my leg as well.' She lifted the dress and pointed to a similar mark on her thigh. She looked up at me apprehensively.

'Don't worry, we'll get that seen to,' I tried to reassure her.

Afterwards, as we walked along the Seine, I took hardly any notice of the two girls. I was too preoccupied with the marks.

Was the little girl sick? Or could they be bruises? Was Idriss beating his daughter? He was sometimes very rough with the girl, and I had witnessed him screaming at her for not doing something the way he wanted on several occasions. But I had never seen any physical violence. Was our beloved Safa not only under threat of mutilation, but also being abused by her father?

I couldn't believe that was true, but I decided to speak to Idriss about it.

However, when we got back to the hotel, he had disappeared again.

'The gentleman went out a good hour ago,' the concierge told me.

I thought he had probably gone looking for the embassy again, but before I had time to worry, Safa began whining

'But I wanted to surprise Papa with my new dress,' she said, pouting.

'Pop upstairs and take the shopping to your room,' I told the girls, 'while I go and look for him.'

Tired and angry at once, I went outside and lit a cigarette. I realised that the events of the past few days, the huge responsibility and the ambitious itinerary for our African guests were starting to take their toll. I peered up and down the street – and in the distance, I thought I could make out Idriss in his luminous orange padded jacket. I screwed up my eyes and started walking quickly in his direction. It really was Safa's father, standing on a street corner and speaking to passers-by. They were looking at him quizzically, then shaking their heads and walking on. What was he doing?

Idriss jumped when he saw me. 'Errr . . .' he stuttered. 'I was asking them for directions,' he said eventually.

'To where? The hotel is just over there – you know that,' I retorted. I had had enough, and took the bull by the horns. 'What is it you're always looking for in Paris? Tell me . . . Maybe I can help you.'

Idriss looked at the ground in embarrassment and

confirmed my suspicions. 'I want to go to the Djibouti Embassy.'

'Why?' I asked, pretending I knew nothing about his plan.

'I want to live in Europe with my family. Everything is so beautiful and clean here. Everyone has money, and people can afford everything they want. I want to live like that too.'

'Idriss,' I sighed. 'I understand. But just coming to Europe wouldn't be the solution to your problems. You would have just as little to live on as you do in Djibouti. And everything here is much, much more expensive than where you live. Even if you could work as a taxi driver in France, your wages wouldn't be enough to feed your whole family. You would still be living in poverty.'

We had reached the entrance to the hotel.

'But I just need one of those cards, like you have,' said Idriss. 'You know: the plastic thing you use to get money from the box in the wall.'

That made me chuckle. Over the past few days I had used my bank card to take money out of my account several times. I could see the reason for his confusion.

We went into the lobby and sat down on a sofa to wait for the girls. I got my wallet out of my bag, took out my bank card and showed it to Idriss, who stared at it as if this piece of plastic was the answer to his prayers. 'Yes, you can use this card to get money out of your account anywhere in the world,' I explained to him. 'But it's not unlimited – you can only take out as much as you have in your account. The boxes in the wall that you've seen are actually a kind of curse.' Idriss looked at me incredulously. 'They make it so easy to withdraw money at any time of day . . . and that means you very quickly have less and less. If you run out of money, the machine stops spitting it out.'

Idriss was deeply disappointed by this information. 'So I have to put money in before I can take it out again?' he asked, and when I nodded he said, 'Well, that's stupid!'

'I think so, too. But that's just the way it is.'

Before we could talk any more about why he wanted to stay, the lift door opened and Safa got out. Her father's face lit up instantly. He admired his little daughter as she showed him her new white dress, spinning round to make the skirt dance. In their room, Inab had put matching clasps in Safa's hair, and the little one looked enchanting. Even Idriss said as much.

We all went to lunch together, and then took another walk along the Seine, because the girls wanted to show Idriss the wonderful river. At the Pont des Arts they admired the railings, which sparkled in the afternoon sun as if they were made of gold. Mesmerised, Inab and Safa ran on to the bridge and waved to us excitedly to come and join them.

'You have to come and look at this!' they called out, pointing at all the padlocks.

The brightly painted little locks adorned the whole length of the wire mesh fence. I knelt down to take a closer look at the brass padlocks, and discovered that they had all been decorated. On every single one there were messages: little hearts, names or wishes written in permanent marker.

'What are they for?' Safa asked inquisitively.

'I think that people who are in love, or have just got married – or best friends, sisters and other people who are happy – come here to seal their love and happiness with one of these locks,' I said.

'And why do they do that?' Safa asked, surprised by this idea.

'Well, the couples probably think it means their love will last a very long time, and the friends hope they will stay friends for ever. They hope their relationship with the person they love will be as indestructible as these locks.'

Meanwhile, Inab and Idriss were walking over to a man who had set up a little stall at the end of the bridge. A few minutes later they came back with one big lock, one smaller one, and some coloured pens.

'Here,' Idriss said, handing me the larger of the two. 'You can buy them from the man. Let's write our names on this one.'

I was astonished at his request: I hadn't thought him the type for such sentimentality. I took the pen and wrote, *Idriss, Inab, Sophie & Safa – friends for ever* on the smooth, gold surface. The other three approved.

'The man says you have to throw one key into the river and keep the other one,' Inab explained.

No sooner said than done: I found a free spot on the railing, attached the lock and threw one of the keys into the water. 'And what are we going to do with the smaller one, Idriss?'

Without saying anything, he took a blue pen from me and slowly wrote, *15 July – Idriss & Safa* on it. Then he took his daughter by the hand and led her to the sparkling railings, where she fastened their little lock. I watched the two of them with a lump in my throat.

'I will always protect you, my only daughter,' Idriss said softly. Then he took Safa's hand, placed the key in her palm, closed it tenderly and kissed her little fist.

'And you are my beloved Papa, for always,' Safa replied solemnly.

A moment later, she swung her arm back and threw the key in a high arc into the waters of the Seine, where it would remain for ever. I suddenly felt ashamed for thinking that Idriss might be responsible for the mark on Safa's face.

Safa loves Paris and her new 'supercool' outfit.

We strolled on to the next bridge, where Safa sat on a stone wall, and I pulled out my camera. Waris had asked me to take as many photos as possible of their stay in Paris – for Safa and her family to remember it by, and for Waris herself. Inab enjoyed having her photo taken; and she didn't want Safa to be the only one in front of the camera. She sneaked into the shot and struck a funny pose just as I pressed the shutter release.

Then Safa turned and swung her legs over the stone wall so that her feet were dangling above the Seine. Just a few centimetres and the little girl would have fallen into the depths. I lunged towards her and dragged her off the wall: 'Safa, that's much too dangerous!'

The little one didn't understand why I was so shocked. 'But what could happen to me? I just want to jump into the water. Waris showed me how to swim in Djibouti.'

I pointed to the huge boats gliding under the bridge. 'You can't swim here,' I explained. 'Imagine if you jumped and landed on one of the boats down there. And jumping into water from this height is terribly painful – it might even kill you. You don't want that, do you?'

Safa gave a sigh that showed she understood, but that I hadn't managed to really scare her.

*The little desert flower is brave, all right,* I thought. But her bravery could potentially put her in danger.

In the light of the afternoon sun, I could see the dark patch under Safa's eye more clearly, particularly as it had now swollen up. When I looked closer, I saw a little pus-filled lump, like a spot. So it was unlikely to be a bruise – but a girl of seven would hardly be getting acne. While Inab and Idriss went off to buy Coke from the supermarket I took her to a modern-looking shop with the word

PHARMACIE written in giant letters above its door. An older man with metal-rimmed glasses and a brilliant white coat was standing behind the glass counter.

'Good-afternoon,' I said politely to the pharmacist, before coming straight to the point. 'Would you be able to tell me what this is?'

I indicated the worrying marks on Safa's face, while the little girl stood frozen to the spot, not daring to move. The gentleman leaned over the counter and examined her face close up.

Safa stared at him. 'You've got your glasses on the wrong way round,' she said. 'They're not supposed to be on the end of your nose, they should be further up, between your eyes. That's what this indentation is for.' She proudly showed him her pink sunglasses, and put them on the way I had shown her.

The pharmacist chuckled and replied in a kindly voice: 'You're absolutely right. But unfortunately my nose is too big, so I have to wear my glasses down there.'

'Oh, right.' Safa contemplated his large nose thoughtfully.

Then the pharmacist turned back to me. '*Madame,* that looks like eczema to me.' His voice suddenly grew more serious. 'Are you washing your daughter properly?' he asked, with a slightly critical undertone.

'She's not my daughter; she's a guest from Djibouti. She and her father only arrived here in Paris a few days ago. The two of them have never been abroad before.'

The pharmacist apologised at once. 'You wouldn't believe the things I see in this job. Now I understand,' he went on. 'I'm afraid, as far as hygiene goes, conditions are very bad in some countries, and a lot of people have this kind of eczema. I'll give you some ointment: please put a thin layer on the little one three times a day. In a few days, the marks should start to disappear. If they don't, you should see a dermatologist.'

I took the ointment gratefully and paid for it.

As we were leaving, Safa spotted a doctor's bag in the window display. 'I want that!' she cried, so loudly that all the other customers turned to look at her.

'What do you need a doctor's bag for?'

'I saw one like that at Dr Acina's once,' the little girl explained. 'It has lots of things in it that Dr Acina uses to help people,' she went on, standing in the doorway of the pharmacy. 'You know, Sophie, when I grow up I want to help other people too. That's why I need this case.'

The pharmacist had come out from behind his counter. 'It's great that you have career plans already,' he said to the seven-year-old.

'Yes: I have to help a whole lot of girls in Djibouti,' Safa answered resolutely. 'Waris and I are going to stop them being circumcised.'

The man in the white coat looked at me in surprise, but I left the statement without comment. In the space of a few days, this little girl had understood more than thousands of adults all over the world.

# 15

# The car journey

## Waris

I had just put my youngest, Leon, to bed. The little lion
fought against his tiredness almost every evening. His
whole life was spent romping about, playing and learning.
Sleeping, on the other hand, seemed to be a kind of tor-
ment for him. But I had finally managed to rock him to
sleep, and could now turn my attention to my work.

Darkness had fallen over Danzig, and the light from my
living room was the only thing illuminating the white
sandy beach outside my house in the former Hanseatic
city. The decision to settle in Poland, far away from the
hubbub of the central European capitals, had been
absolutely right. It wasn't the first time I had thought it.
Here, I could leave my cares behind, take a break from the

energy-sapping battle against FGM I had been fighting for years, and watch my own sons and my two adopted children, Mo and Hawo, grow up in peace.

I opened my laptop and came to an email from Joanna.

Dear Waris,

Good news from Munich: you've been invited to go there at the end of July to receive the Thomas Dehler Prize, which they want to give you for your work in combating FGM. Isn't that great? If you like, you can invite Safa and the others to the prize-giving. Let's talk about it on the phone tomorrow.

All the best

Joanna

I was delighted at this news. Every year, the Thomas Dehler Stiftung in Germany honoured people who 'fight the enemies of freedom'; I liked that. Not because I am crazy about receiving prizes and awards, but because the prize-giving would draw people's attention back to the foundation and our important work. Of course I would accept the invitation, and I was very pleased that Joanna had suggested taking our guests along. Once I had responded to a few more emails, I fell into bed, exhausted.

'Waris, Waris!'

Safa runs towards me, beaming with joy, across a white-sand beach. Her hair is flying in the wind. She is wearing a pretty, brilliant-white dress, and the hand of Fatima is dangling around her throat as usual.

'You've finally come back to Djibouti.'

I hug her tightly and kiss her on the forehead.

'We're going to help Inab,' I whisper quietly in her ear.

Suddenly I am no longer kneeling in the sand, but in a brightly lit corridor. I stand up, feeling confused. Men and women in white coats walk past me. I speak to them, asking them where I am. But they don't hear me. I walk quickly along the corridor, past countless white doors. I open one after another, and cast a searching glance into the rooms, in each of which are four hospital beds. Young girls and women are lying in them – I don't know them, but they all smile and wave at me.

'Hello, Waris,' they call out happily.

I am quite obviously in a hospital. I walk and walk – there seems to be no end to the long corridor. A feeling I can't put my finger on is drawing me towards a large door in the far distance. I know I have to get there, though I'm not sure why.

'Waris!' a familiar voice suddenly rings out.

It's Inab.

'Inab, where are you?' I call frantically, starting to run.

When I finally reach the large door, I pull it open with some force. The walls of the room are brightly painted, and exude an incredible joy. Inside, there is Inab in a giant bed.

But before I can speak to the girl, a man with greying hair appears beside me. I recognise him, but I just can't place him. I look at his white doctor's coat and try to read what is written there, but I can't. The letters only come into focus when I go right up to him. They spell out DR PIERRE FOLDÈS – and underneath are the words DESERT FLOWER CENTRE.

\*

'Waris, Waris!'

Somebody was shaking my hand, and I sat up with a start. Half asleep, I stared wide-eyed at my adopted daughter Hawo.

'Where am I?' I exclaimed breathlessly.

'We're at home, in Poland. You were dreaming,' the fifteen-year-old girl said. 'I just wanted to let you know that Leon's awake.'

While Hawo padded back to her room, I remained lying in the dark by myself for a few moments. *Pierre Foldès*, I thought, remembering the name I had just seen in my intense dream.

He was a man I knew in real life: a famous French medic who for the past twelve years had specialised in the surgical reconstruction of the vagina and clitoris following genital mutilation. He now helped around 200 women gain a new life every year. Pierre Foldès existed in real life – unlike the Desert Flower Centre hospital, as I had just seen it in my dream. There was no such institution.

'Not yet, that is,' I said out loud to myself, before going next door to check on Leon.

In the morning I called my manager and confidant Walter, managing to catch him at the airport where he was waiting for his flight to Paris. He was the most important man in the Desert Flower Foundation, which we had set up together. Like me, he was convinced that we should extend the scope of our work, and for the past few months he had been laying the groundwork for several Desert Flower centres, where we wanted to offer reconstructive surgery to girls who had undergone genital mutilation. When he had told me of his plan for the first time, I had thrown my arms around him. I loved him for the enthusiasm he had for our work, and the fact that he always thought big. He too lived by the saying 'There's no such word as "can't".' Over the last few years, this motto and our boundless energy had brought the Desert Flower Foundation so far, and I was sure it would take the organisation much further in the years to come.

But for now, Walter was on his way to France, to drive our friends Inab, Idriss and Safa across Europe in a minibus. Of course, it would have been simpler to put them on a plane to Vienna. But we wanted to show them more than just airports and big cities. We wanted them to experience the landscapes of this place that was so far from their home continent.

Our plan paid off.

# Walter

'Everything is so beautifully green here,' said Idriss, who was sitting in the front passenger seat next to me, a good three hours into the trip.

Since Sophie and I had loaded the group into the car in Paris, Idriss had not spoken a word. He had simply watched the lush French countryside roll by in silence. He now started chatting to me about France and Djibouti.

Inab, who was sitting behind them next to Sophie, had fallen asleep, and in the seat behind them Safa had nodded off as well, her earphones still in her ears. Sophie eased the iPod out of the girl's hand and covered her with her jacket.

At the start of the journey, Safa had turned the music up as loud as she could. Soon the little one was singing raucously along with the songs, although she didn't speak a word of English. She liked 'Get Lucky' by Daft Punk so much that she played it several times in a row. From then on, she refused to let go of the iPod.

After another hour had gone by, Sophie glanced at Inab and Safa, who were now awake and squirming impatiently in their seats, before leaning forward and asking: 'Could we maybe stop for a break?'

'Yes, of course, we're low on petrol in any case.'

I pulled into the next service station. While I filled the car, Sophie took the girls to the toilet, and a jittery Idriss lit a cigarette. The smoking ban in the hire car seemed to be taking its toll on him.

As they had feared, the ladies' toilet was hopelessly crowded.

'But I really need to go!' Safa whined.

Without further ado, the three of them went into the men's. While Inab disappeared into one cubicle, Sophie headed into the other one with Safa.

'No, wait outside!' Safa said sternly, pushing Sophie out.

'But Safa, we're both girls. I'm not going to look,' Sophie replied, not understanding her reluctance.

Safa panicked. 'Stay outside!' she shouted, slamming the door.

'Is everything OK?' Sophie asked anxiously when Safa came out of the toilet – as always, without having flushed it. Sophie did it for her, and asked again: 'Are you OK?'

The girl lowered her eyes. 'Yes,' she said hesitantly.

Sophie wasn't sure if she could believe her. She decided

to find a quiet moment to ask me when Dr Acina had last examined the little one. A few months had passed since Waris's visit to Djibouti, when the paediatrician had confirmed that Safa had not yet been cut – and a lot could happen in a few months.

Safa's uncertainty was instantly banished when she and Inab were washing their hands, and they discovered the sensor that turned on the taps.

'Look, we can do magic.' She waved her hands back and forth excitedly, switching the water on and off.

'Hey, come and look at this!' Inab exclaimed, putting both hands into the electric hand dryer as the little sign instructed her. With a loud roar, it blew out warm air.

Safa squealed in delight and copied her.

When the three of them returned to the car, Idriss was standing by a bin, smoking his final cigarette before we drove on.

As she was getting in, Sophie's gaze fell on the open crisp packets, crumbs, empty water bottles and apple cores littering the floor and seats. She hurriedly gathered up the rubbish and took it to the bin.

'Please pull yourselves together,' she scolded them indignantly. 'This is a hire car; it doesn't belong to us. This isn't how you treat things that aren't yours.'

Safa and Inab climbed wordlessly into the car and watched as Sophie fished out the empty packaging from under the seats. As she was picking up an orange juice bottle, its cap came off, and the contents spurted all over Inab's feet and shoes.

The eighteen-year-old cried out: 'Help, my new shoes!' She had been so proud of the pretty high heels, and now they were ruined.

Embarrassed, Sophie pulled off Inab's shoes and emptied the orange juice out of them before hurrying to the toilet to sponge them off.

When she came back, she immediately trod in a little lake.

'Eeuw!' Sophie exclaimed, lifting her feet.

The carpet in the footwell was saturated with orange juice. Everyone grinned, though nobody said anything. Then Safa leaned forward.

'Sophie, this is a hire car,' the little one said, imitating her. 'You need to take care of things that aren't yours!'

'You're right: one-nil to you,' Sophie admitted, quickly mopping up the liquid so we could get going again.

Just over three hours later, we reached Munich. As the group entered the hotel, the receptionist eyed the three Africans suspiciously.

'Are they with you?' he asked Sophie rudely.

Sophie would have liked to turn on her heel that instant and leave the hotel and its xenophobic staff. But after a glance at the exhausted faces of Inab, Safa and her father, she decided just to ignore him.

'We need a completed check-in form for each guest,' the receptionist said, putting five forms on the desk.

Sophie and I began to fill in the forms straight away, while Inab and Idriss just stared at theirs, feeling out of their depth.

'Your name goes here,' explained Sophie, who now knew that Idriss could write his own name. 'And your date of birth goes here.'

But Idriss didn't know exactly when he had been born. Under the receptionist's contemptuous gaze, Sophie took the African's passport and copied out his date of birth.

'This line is for the name of the street you live on,' Sophie went on.

'Balbala,' said Idriss tersely.

'I know that,' replied Sophie, 'but what street do you live on?'

Safa's father shrugged.

'There are hardly any street names in Djibouti. And none at all in Balbala,' I said.

'But we do need some kind of information,' the receptionist remarked unsympathetically.

Without saying anything, Sophie wrote: *Main Road, Balbala* in the address box.

Sophie was in a good mood the next morning when she came into the breakfast room to find me there, sipping a cup of coffee.

'Aren't you having anything to eat?' she asked.

'No, I'm still full from dinner last night.'

Late the previous evening we had found a Turkish restaurant that was still open. The friendly owner had served us fresh lamb with delicious sauces and plenty of sides. It was quite a heavy meal to have eaten so soon before bed.

'Where are the girls and Idriss?'

'I'm sure they'll be down in a minute. He's hardly going to go looking for the Djibouti Embassy here in Munich,' Sophie laughed, and told me about what had happened in Paris. 'Although I'm not sure we're going to be able to put him off the idea altogether.'

Before I could reply, Safa's father entered the room, without the girls. Sophie got up to check on them.

When Inab opened the door to their room, Sophie couldn't believe her eyes. In the space of a few hours the two of them had wreaked complete havoc there. The carpet was covered in papers, clothes, price lists and food leftovers. The bathroom floor was submerged under a centimetre of water, although the shower obviously hadn't been used.

'What on earth have you been doing in here?' Sophie cried as she entered the room. She demanded that the girls, who were completely taken aback, make everything spotless again before they came down to breakfast.

Inab and Safa stood to attention in front of her like little soldiers and answered: 'Yes, Sophie!'

On the way back down to the restaurant, Sophie regretted being so strict with the girls. She was well aware that they had never had a room of their own to keep tidy. The shacks where they lived with their parents were so small that you couldn't leave anything lying around. She sat down and drank her coffee thoughtfully, while Idriss and I talked about Munich.

Half an hour later Inab and Safa finally appeared, proudly reporting that their room was now pristine. The breakfast buffet had been cleared away by this point, but to be on the safe side Sophie had already fetched the girls some eggs, bread rolls and fruit juice. She had ordered herself another coffee, and was reaching for the sugar pot when Safa grabbed it to put on her eggs.

'Safa, that's not salt – it's sugar,' she warned the little one, who calmly carried on trickling the white granules on to her scrambled eggs. She started to eat contentedly.

'You don't have to eat that,' said Sophie. She tried to remember whether the Somali had eaten eggs in Paris.

Safa, meanwhile, simply carried on munching. 'Is it good?' Sophie asked in disbelief, as I laughed.

'Yes, it's very good actually.'

Then Inab put in: 'We eat eggs with sugar at home. Some people prefer salt; others like sugar. Each to his own.'

Idriss agreed with her, and Sophie and I looked at each other in surprise.

'Go on, try some. It's really delicious,' Safa suggested, having almost cleared her plate.

We two Austrians thanked her, but declined.

A short while later, once I had been out to fetch the car, we all checked out. The unfriendly receptionist only shook hands with Sophie and me in parting, simply ignoring the dark-skinned guests. Whilst Sophie was indignant, I, sadly, was no longer surprised by situations like this. I had experienced them too often before on my trips for the foundation.

'We'll be in Vienna in just a few hours,' Sophie announced grandly, like an airline pilot to people boarding a plane. 'On the way, you'll see Austria's incredible landscape. We have a lot of mountains.'

As we passed over the border between Germany and Austria, Safa's father asked in amazement: 'Why aren't there any border patrols here? Don't we have to show our passports and let them search our luggage?'

I explained the principle of the European Union to him.

'So everyone can travel back and forth between the different countries as he pleases?' Idriss said incredulously.

'Yes, if you're an EU citizen,' Sophie said. She could imagine what Safa's father had in mind. 'But non-EU citizens need a residence permit in order to make use of

that right. Look, those are the Alps up ahead.' Sophie
pointed out of the window in an effort to move off this sensitive subject.

The awe-inspiring crags rose up in front of them into a
pale blue sky. Safa, Idriss and Inab pressed their noses flat
against the car windows and admired the majestic mountains, whose snow-capped peaks stood out from the lush
green valleys below.

'It's so beautiful,' Inab said softly. 'Do you live here?'

Sophie laughed. 'No, I live in Vienna, but my dad comes
from a mountain like this. See how high it is? That's nearly
three thousand metres,' she explained. 'As a child, my dad
used to go to school on skis in the winter; he would ski
down from the mountain into the valley.'

Safa looked at her with big, questioning eyes. 'What are
skis?'

Sophie struggled to find the right words, and I helped
her out. 'They're two planks that you strap under your
feet, and you can slide over the snow on them.'

Sophie added: 'It's great fun. You can go really fast; it's
a bit like riding a rollercoaster, like you did in Paris.'

Safa clapped her hands excitedly. 'I'd like to try that too.
Can we go skiing tomorrow ... please?' she cried.

I had to explain that you could only ski in winter. 'But
I'm sure you'll come and visit us again, and then we'll
teach you.'

Idriss liked the idea too. He was still gazing in fascination at the mountains. 'I'd like to learn as well,' he said
quietly. 'Is it true that snow is very cold?'

'Ice-cold,' said Sophie.

Everyone remained lost in their own thoughts until we
reached the Mondsee. The sun was beating down on the

roof of the red mini-van, and the air-conditioning was
struggling to combat the baking heat. From the motorway
we could see the deep-blue lake, where glittering waves
danced across the surface of the water.

'The sea, the sea!' Safa cried, and at once asked impatiently: 'When are we going swimming? I brought the
swimming costume Waris bought me specially.'

I threw Sophie a meaningful look in the rear-view
mirror. 'I've got a great idea,' I said. 'Let's turn off here
and have a quick dip in the lake.'

Safa and Inab cheered, and Idriss also seemed to be glad
of the chance to freshen up and have a cigarette. I turned
off the motorway, and a few minutes later we pulled up at
the public beach, where dozens of children and young
people were playing and larking about.

On the way to the changing rooms, Sophie realised that
this was another chance for her to find out whether Safa
was still intact. Since the girl's worrying outburst in the
service station toilets, Sophie hadn't been able to shake
her worries.

But once again, the child wouldn't let Sophie in. 'You
stay outside and make sure nobody comes,' Safa said
firmly, leaving the cubicle door open just a tiny crack.

Inab got changed quickly. She didn't own a bathing suit,
and so had just thrown on a T-shirt and shorts. Safa, on the
other hand, was taking for ever.

'Help, I'm stuck!' the little desert flower groaned from
inside the changing cubicle.

Sophie cautiously opened the door and saw that Safa
had put the swimming costume on the wrong way round,
and her plaits were now caught on one of the straps.
Laughing, Sophie freed her trapped hair, whereupon Safa

suddenly started screeching hysterically and trying to cover her bare chest with her arms.

Sophie glanced outside, where an old man was walking past. 'Safa, that man's just passing, he didn't even look in – and anyway, it's only your top half that's naked,' she tried to reassure the little one.

'Hurry up and get dressed,' Inab snapped at the little girl from outside, and then carried on scolding her in Somali.

Sophie left the cubicle and closed the door behind her, sad that the girls' upbringing had robbed them of their freedom.

Inab ran past her towards the jetty, with Safa in her wake. Sophie followed the girls down to the glass-clear lake, while Idriss and I had a cup of coffee in the beach restaurant.

Inab dipped her toes cautiously in the water. 'Brr, it's too cold for me,' she declared, sitting down next to Sophie, who was also dangling her legs in the cool water.

Safa flitted past them and, before the two women had time to react, fearlessly sprang head-first into the lake, creating a huge splash. She surfaced again, coughing, and spent the next hour playing contentedly with the other children. When it was time to set off, the adults were only able to coax her out of the water with the promise that they would go swimming again in Vienna.

Back in the car, she sulked until they passed a small wind farm at the side of the road.

'What's that?' Safa tapped Sophie on the shoulder and pointed at the large windmills towering into the sky above the shining yellow and green fields.

Idriss listened intently as Sophie and I explained how

they created electricity. 'That would be a great thing for Djibouti,' he said. 'In Balbala hardly anyone has access to electricity, but almost everyone has a mobile or some other device. They could charge them at my house. And I wouldn't make them pay very much, and so in the end everyone would get something out of it. I would just need a windmill like that.'

As dream-like as his idea sounded, there was definitely something in it. People don't realise that starvation isn't the only cause of premature death in the developing world; a lot of people also suffer fatal lung diseases caused by burning everything they can get their hands on, from plastic bags to aluminium cans.

'Where do you cook: in the house or outside?' Sophie asked Safa's father.

'Most people cook in the house. We have an open kitchen, and now we have a kerosene stove. It's inside, against a wall, but on the other side it's open, so the smoke can escape.'

Idriss was obviously aware that cooking with kerosene was bad for people's health.

'But you know a lot of children get sick from that?' Sophie pressed him.

'Well, yes, it's obvious the smoke isn't healthy,' he replied. 'The fact that there are so many children with lung problems where we live might well be due to the fireplaces in the houses.'

'And what about Amir?' Sophie said, unwilling to let the matter drop. 'Could that have made him sick, too?'

Idriss dismissed this. 'No, that can't be it. He was never exposed to the smoke for very long, and now we cook practically in the open.'

Sophie gazed out of the window thoughtfully. Of course it was perfectly possible that the little one's illness might have another cause. But all the indications were that Amir too had been poisoned by the terrible conditions in the slums. Idriss seemed reluctant to acknowledge it – but that was completely understandable. He would otherwise have had to blame himself for his child's serious health condition.

'Wake up! We're in Vienna!'

I startled the passengers, who had all nodded off. For the first time in hours the car slowed down, and stopped at the first set of traffic lights inside the city limits. Sophie was glad to be home at last, after this short but demanding trip. Inab and Safa rubbed their eyes. In the light of this balmy summer evening, the beautiful Schönbrunn Palace, which we were just passing, shone an even more intense yellow than usual.

'Am I dreaming, or is that house really there?' asked Inab, who had only just opened her eyes.

Sophie and I laughed.

'That's a real palace. It's one of the many wonderful sights we're going to visit in the next few days.'

Idriss, Inab and Safa were soon standing in front of the hotel where Sophie had reserved two rooms for them. To their surprise, they were going to be left to their own devices for the first time in days.

'Aren't you going to stay in the hotel with us again?' Safa asked as Sophie showed the three of them to their rooms.

Sophie had to disappoint her. 'Walter and I both live in Vienna, so we're going to sleep at home.'

'Can't we come and stay with you, then?' Inab asked.

'I would love you to, but I'm afraid I don't have room. You can come and visit me any time though.' In European terms, Sophie's flat was tiny. But for Inab and Safa, it would have been a palace compared with their huts.

'Oh, yeah!' Safa exclaimed. 'We'll come over tomorrow, then.'

The little one stood on tiptoes to give Sophie a kiss on the arm, and said affectionately, 'I love you, Sophie.'

'I love you too. You two promise me you'll behave yourselves, OK?' she said to the girls in parting. Then she turned to Safa's father. 'Idriss, I'm relying on you to look after the pair of them. My colleague will come and pick you up in the morning – I'll see you in the office.'

Inab and Safa gazed sadly out of the window of their room at the red minivan as Sophie and I drove away. A new phase of their trip had begun.

# 16

# Excitement in Vienna

## Sophie

The Vienna office of the Desert Flower Foundation was a hive of activity. Inab and Safa looked inquisitively around the rooms of the old building. The walls were covered in pictures of Walter, Joanna and Waris on their travels, and attending various events.

'But that's Africa!' Safa cried, overjoyed to see a picture of Waris in the desert with an African family.

'Yes, that's right, Safa,' I confirmed. The little one had leapt into my arms as soon as she had seen me.

Inab scrutinised the shelves of files. 'Did you write all those?' she said. 'That must have been a lot of work.'

My colleague Juliana had made coffee for Idriss. Safa's father looked tired as he sat down on an office chair at my large desk. He slurped his coffee and asked if he could smoke.

'No, sorry,' I said. 'Walter is a non-smoker, and he doesn't like it.'

I moved my mouse. With a quiet hum, the Desert Flower Foundation logo, my screensaver, vanished, and a picture appeared of Safa's family on the veranda in Balbala, taken a few months previously.

'*Ma chérie!*' Idriss exclaimed when he spotted his wife in the photo. 'I miss her so much!' His eyes began to fill with tears.

I clicked on the printer symbol, and a few seconds later a colour print-out of the picture appeared from the machine next to my desk. I handed it to Idriss, and he ran his fingers over the photo, which also showed his two sons Amir and Nour.

Then I opened another folder of pictures and showed them to Idriss and Safa, who had come to see what was going on.

Juliana called Inab over to her. 'Come and sit with me, and help me with my work.'

The eighteen-year-old was delighted by the invitation – and there was a specific reason Juliana had made it. While Inab was in Vienna, we wanted to find out whether she knew enough to eventually head up the Desert Flower Foundation's office in Djibouti. Inab spoke very good French, but we still had to check whether the spoken and written English she had learned at school was up to scratch. A good grasp of English was essential for working in an international organisation.

Juliana opened a blank Word document and said to Inab, 'Could you write a few lines in English, please?'

'What shall I write?' the girl asked hesitantly.

'Maybe you could write a letter to ... ' Juliana thought for a moment. 'Sophie.'

Inab training at the Desert Flower Foundation headquarters in Vienna.

Inab started to type, tentatively at first, but with growing confidence. She was soon hammering away at the keys.

A few minutes later, Juliana printed the document and gave it to me to read.

Hello,

My name is Inab, I am eighteen years old, I have a brother and two sisters and I am from Djibouti. I love Europe. Thank you for inviting me.

Sophie, I want to tell you that you are my friend and that I love you. I want to work in the office and I want to be a business woman.

I love you,

Inab

The girl gave me a shy smile before sitting back down at Juliana's desk and watching her type an email.

'And you are my friend and I love you too,' I said in English. At that moment, I had a strong feeling that the girl would soon become a colleague.

While Idriss went outside for a cigarette, Safa and I looked at more photos on my computer. The girl followed my every move attentively.

'What's that?' she asked.

'That's called a mouse,' I explained to her. 'You use it to work the computer.'

'But it only has a tail; it doesn't have any ears.'

I couldn't but be touched by the way Safa was discovering the world. 'Do you recognise the girl in this photo?' I asked, opening an image file from the filming of *Desert Flower*. It showed the three-year-old Safa, whose large, expressive eyes had moved an audience of millions.

'That's me!' the little desert flower cried in delight.

I seized the chance to ask the girl some questions. 'Do you remember making the film?'

Safa shook her head. 'Not really. I just know I was very scared sometimes.'

'You mean when they were filming the circumcision scene, and you screamed really loudly?'

Safa nodded. I held the little girl tightly and looked deep into her eyes. 'But you know what they did to Waris is never going to happen to you, right?' I asked, hoping against hope that the little one would reassure me it hadn't been done already.

But before Safa could say anything, the doorbell rang.

Liat, a designer who had created a line of jewellery to support the foundation, had dropped by to present some new pieces. Safa's father was standing beside her.

'I found this gentleman outside,' Liat said to Juliana with a smile as she opened the office door. 'I take it he's with you.'

The stylishly dressed jeweller introduced herself to everyone, and then opened the little suitcase she had brought with her. Inside, her new designs shimmered against a black velvet cushion.

Inab and Safa, who were standing right next to her, both let out a cry of amazement: 'Wow!'

'Is that all real gold?' Safa whispered.

'Yes, it's real gold,' Liat replied in her lovely, rich accent. 'But you're wearing a pretty piece like that round your neck as well.' The designer pointed to the gold hand of Fatima shining against Safa's dark skin.

The girl's eyes didn't move a millimetre from the jewellery case, with its rows of gorgeous creations. Liat carefully lifted out the first compartment, under which another layer of lovely designs came into view. The girls could hardly believe it.

Liat took out one of the necklaces. 'Look, it's just like yours.'

Safa stared in fascination at the pendant dangling in front of her face, as if she was being hypnotised. It was another hand of Fatima. The artist told Safa that she had made the necklace Waris had given her. It was the proto-type for a collection that featured this special sign, which was supposed to protect its wearer for ever.

The little desert flower proudly put her hand to her throat. 'If Waris gave me something that valuable, it must mean she really loves me, mustn't it?' she asked tentatively.

Liat stroked her soft cheek and said: 'You can be very, very sure of that.'

I rang Waris as soon as I could.

'I'm terribly afraid that Safa might have been cut in the last few months,' I whispered.

'What are you saying?'

I told Waris about the events that had led me to this ter-rible suspicion. 'It feels like somebody has told her not to let us see her naked.'

Waris told me she remembered that evening in Djibouti when Fozia had suggested that the family couldn't stand the social pressure any longer, and would one day have to make Safa a 'pure girl'. Had this woman really carried out her threat? The fact that Safa wasn't in pain made me think she hadn't, but we had to know for sure as soon as possible.

I could hear Waris take a deep breath. She said firmly: 'Sophie, I have to speak to Idriss at once.'

My plan to keep Idriss back to phone Waris failed utterly, however, as he was insistent on going with the girls and Juliana, leaving me on my own in the office.

Juliana drove the three Africans into the city. She showed them the Stadtpark and took them along Kärntner Straße to St Stephen's Cathedral. Then they strolled through the pedestrianised zone to buy Inab a swimming costume. Juliana was hoping that Safa would try one on as well, and she would get a chance to check she was still intact. Although the temperature was a good thirty degrees, Idriss stubbornly refused to take off his padded jacket. Smoking, he trudged along behind Juliana as the girls skipped along happily; the heat hardly seemed to bother him.

When Juliana returned to the Desert Flower Foundation office without them, two hours later, I was still sitting at my desk, staring at photos of Safa in Paris on my computer screen.

'Where are the others?' I asked impatiently. 'Did you manage to find out if Safa is OK?'

Looking defeated, Juliana reported that she had quarrelled with Safa's father in the department store while Inab was trying on shorts and sports bras. She had tried to convince Inab to look at one-piece swimming costumes or bikinis, but the girl was clearly uncomfortable at the very idea of showing skin. And as a Muslim, Idriss was firmly against the girls wearing anything too revealing.

'Honestly, I was just glad to get out of the shop. And I'm afraid I wasn't able to do anything about Safa.' She sounded contrite. 'Now the three of them have gone to the hotel to rest.'

Disappointed, I gazed at the image on my monitor: Safa beaming happily at the fairground in Paris, excited and carefree.

'I honestly can't imagine that Safa has been cut. She is so happy, and there's no sign whatsoever that she's in pain,' I said, thinking aloud. 'But that still doesn't completely set my mind at rest.'

On the spur of the moment, I dialled Waris in Poland.

'Waris, Idriss might be alone in his hotel room now, so you could speak to him without any interruptions.'

# Waris

'Hello, Idriss?'

I hadn't hesitated for a second before calling Safa's father. I was desperate to know the truth – no matter how terrible it was.

The man seemed perturbed. 'Waris? Waris Dirie?'

When I had managed to convince him it was really me on the end of the line, I opened with some polite conversation. 'So, how are you all doing? Do you like Europe?' I asked as innocently as I could.

Idriss, by contrast, got straight down to business. 'I'm glad you've called me, Waris,' he said in Somali. 'We like Europe very much. And we would like to stay here for ever.'

Sophie had already explained to him that this would be far from simple, but her words had clearly had no impact at all.

'Idriss,' I said, trying to be patient, 'we'll see each other in Germany in a few days. Then we'll have plenty of time to talk all this through. But before that, I have to ask you an important question.' I paused for a moment and took a deep breath. 'I'm going to be awarded a prize for my work, and I would like to take you all with me to the ceremony in Munich. I'm being honoured for my fight against FGM, Idriss. You know how important my work is to me, don't you?'

At first, Safa's father didn't understand what I was getting at, and just said, 'Yes, sure.'

'Sophie says that on your trip there have been a few times when Safa has behaved very strangely. Idriss,' I said in my mother tongue, stressing his name, 'has your daughter been circumcised since our last visit to Djibouti?'

Several seconds went by. To me they seemed like minutes, hours ...

Eventually he replied. 'What makes you think that? And what do you mean by Safa behaving strangely? She's been no different from usual,' Idriss snorted indignantly into the phone.

I tried to work out from the tone of his voice whether he was feeling guilty, or just offended that I didn't trust him.

'We have a contract, Waris, and we have always stuck to it. We need the food and the money you send us.'

I slowly let out a breath which it felt like I had been holding for several minutes. I was fairly sure Safa's father wasn't lying to me.

'That's good: I just wanted to know,' I said with some relief, before trying to start a conversation about something more trivial. But Idriss had had enough: 'Was that all?' Before I could reply, he snapped: 'Right then. We'll see each other in a few days, and then we can talk about the contract again. Have a nice evening.'

Speechless, I sat there holding the phone to my ear, although in his hotel room in Vienna Idriss had already hung up. The most important question had been answered: Safa, my beloved little desert flower, was still intact. However, I knew deep down that my fight to save her was not over yet. Idriss had shown his true colours when he had said that his family needed the money and food the foundation provided every month. Safa's parents still weren't convinced of the cruelty and senselessness of female genital mutilation. They were sparing their daughter for purely economic reasons.

And now that Idriss knew how much I cared that his daughter remained intact, he was sure to try to use that.

'Then we can talk about the contract again,' he had announced. I was certain that he was going to demand more from us in return for guaranteeing that nothing would happen to the little one. Of course, his motive wouldn't be hate or revenge, but his own poverty – although that didn't improve the situation I had just got myself into one iota. I had opened myself up.

## Sophie

I was hugely relieved by the good news, and managed to sleep soundly for the first time in days. I was well rested the next morning when Walter and I drove our three guests out to the Schneeberg, in nearby lower Austria, where there is an idyllic waterfall.

The mountain road wound through thick green forests, up to a clearing where an old, painted wooden farmhouse stood in the bright sunshine. A narrow stream ran along one side of it.

Idriss took an audible deep breath as he got out of the car. The fresh mountain climate was a far cry from the sticky summer heat in the city centre. Without waiting for the others, he ran to the edge of the stream, knelt down and put both hands into the cold, glass-clear water.

'Safa, come here,' he called out to his daughter. 'Can you smell the water and the earth?' He let the sparkling droplets of water dance over his dark hands in the sunlight.

'I've never seen such lovely clear water,' Safa said in hushed tones. 'Look at it glittering – and it smells fresh.' She slipped off her new trainers, and a minute later was standing in the stream with the water swirling round her ankles. Her childish squeals drew Inab, Walter and me over to them.

'It's ice-cold!' she shouted.

'Can you drink this water?' Safa's father asked.

I bent down, cupped my hands and drank a few mouthfuls.

'So you can just come here any time you're thirsty?' said Idriss.

I explained to him that in Austria you could drink tap water without a second thought as well, because it was basically the same as the water in the stream.

'But the water that comes out of the shower can't be drinking water, can it?' Idriss replied, taken aback.

'Yes, it is,' I said, feeling slightly ashamed.

'Can we talk about food instead now?' Inab joked. 'I'm getting hungry.'

And so we put off our walk until later, and settled down on the rustic wooden veranda of the farmhouse, which also housed a restaurant.

'My Fozia would like it here,' said Idriss, out of the blue. Until this point, he had hardly mentioned his *chérie*, as he called her. But he wasn't the only one who was saddened by the thought of their families sitting in their meagre huts in Djibouti while they were filling their bellies here in paradise. Safa suddenly looked deflated.

'At least you know your mother is waiting for you. You can be glad of that,' Inab pointed out. It really wasn't certain whether Inab's mother would be there when she got back.

'So why did your mother leave?' asked Walter, who, unlike me, didn't know the story.

'She was sick,' the eighteen-year-old replied. 'And my father was sometimes rough with her.'

'You never told me that, Inab,' I said. 'What made him abuse your mother?'

Idriss didn't understand why she was so upset. 'But it's got nothing to do with abuse,' he butted in. 'The Qur'an allows men to hit their wives and children.'

'Idriss, nothing in the world gives somebody the right to be violent towards other people. No matter if it's men, women or children,' I argued, as Walter nodded vigorously in agreement.

'Well, I never said I hit *ma chérie*. Calm down,' Idriss said in an attempt to set our minds at rest.

But the look in Safa's eyes made us wonder whether this time her father was telling the truth.

After a nice long break, we set off along a hiking trail.

While Walter, Idriss and Safa strode off up the mountain, Inab and I hung back a little.

'I'm so frightened for my sisters,' Inab said, seizing the opportunity. 'Our neighbours and friends get cross with me for stopping them being circumcised. I hope they don't do anything to the two of them while I'm away.' She told me that the teachers were always threatening to ban the girls from Qur'an lessons because they were 'impure'. 'I tell them that we pay the school. You know, with the money from the foundation. If they aren't allowed in the Qur'an lessons, I say, then I'll take my sisters out of school and demand my money back on the spot.'

*How incredibly brave and mature this young woman is*, I thought.

Seeing that the others had already disappeared from view, we sat down on a bench at the edge of the path.

'Do your sisters actually know what FGM is? Do they know exactly what you're protecting them from?' I asked cautiously.

Inab fidgeted on the bench. 'Yes – I told them my story. Do you want to hear it?' The young woman raised her head, to see whether I was strong enough to hear what she was about to say.

I nodded silently.

'One day, when I was little, my mother took me with her to the neighbours' house. There were already a lot of girls gathered there, and there were all kinds of treats – popcorn, Coca-Cola, sweets – as if it was a big party. I was only six years old, but I still have a vivid memory of the terrible screams coming from the dark room where the old cutter-woman was torturing one little girl after another. I didn't know exactly what was happening in there, but I knew I didn't want it to happen to me. Some of the girls weren't even four years old.'

Inab took a deep breath and exhaled again. The memory of the horrific scenes had brought tears to her eyes.

'When one of the mothers carried her screaming toddler out, I caught a glimpse of the dark room.' Inab's voice wavered. 'Everything was covered in blood. A lake of it had formed on the floor, where the ugly old woman was kneeling with a razor blade in her hand, waiting for her next victim. Even the walls were sprayed with blood.'

I covered my face. Of course I had heard and read a lot about female genital mutilation in the course of my work for the foundation, and had even written about it – but hearing it first-hand, I was as shocked by Inab's story as if I was one of the millions of people worldwide who have never heard about this horror.

'Then they tried to catch me and take me into the room as well,' Inab went on. 'And at first, I was too quick. I raced outside and ran off as fast as I could. But my mother came after me and eventually caught me. She grabbed me by the arm and some other women helped her drag me back into the house. I tried to tear myself loose, but I couldn't. So I fell on the floor, and shouted and screamed until they gave up.'

'And then one day, they did it anyway . . . ' I said

'Yes. I was thirteen. I had managed to defend myself for years, but by then I just didn't have the strength for it any more. I kind of passed out as I lay on the floor in the dingy room, waiting for the cutter-woman to pull out her blade.'

Inab started to cry bitterly, and helplessly I put my arms around her again.

'Sophie, I'll never, ever forget that moment. The fear; the pain.'

It was only after several minutes that she started to pull herself together, and wiped her face with the back of her hand.

Then she sobbed: 'And ever since, I've known that something that hurts so much can't be the will of Allah. I'm sure of it!'

'But Waris promised you we're going to help you, remember?' I asked.

The eighteen-year-old nodded, and listened with rapt attention as I told her how the reconstructive surgery worked. 'Dr Foldès can rebuild a clitoris in just over half an hour. He uses a laser to remove the scar tissue. The heat of the laser beam means there's hardly any bleeding. Then he pulls the clitoris, which reaches deep into the body, out a little way, and sews up the wound.'

'And how long are you sick for afterwards?' Inab asked, staring at me in disbelief.

'The women can go home the same day. Afterwards, they can even feel things again.'

'How do you mean?' Inab asked quietly, a note of embarrassment in her voice.

'You know,' I said, 'sleeping with a man can be a very beautiful thing, Inab. This doctor could give you back the sensations that have been stolen from you.'

Inab looked thoughtfully at the ground.

'Think about it: if you want to have the operation, we can arrange it. Soon.'

The young woman straightened up and looked at me. 'I trust you – and Waris, Walter and the whole Desert Flower team,' she said. 'If it can really be done, then nothing's going to stop me having the operation.'

# 17

# The training session

On the journey back to Vienna from the Schneeberg, Walter and I decided to hold an impromptu training session the following day.

First thing in the morning, I positioned a flip chart in front of the large sofa in our office. A pile of French books and brochures about FGM lay on the table.

Idriss, Inab and Safa were sitting in a row like school-children, waiting expectantly. The girls giggled in excitement.

'Today I'm going to tell you about the work that Waris and the Desert Flower Foundation do.'

First, I explained the various different methods that were used for the cruel ritual in the different regions of Africa. 'When only the clitoris is removed, it's called a clitoridectomy.' I wrote the word on the board.

'Like what happened to me,' said Inab quietly. Safa gave her a sympathetic look.

'When the inner labia are cut off as well, either partly or completely,' I went on, 'that's called excision.'

I looked at Idriss, who was listening with interest. Airing this topic in front of an African man, particularly with his young daughter in the room, was no simple matter, and I was finding it difficult to anticipate his reactions.

'Very often, the outer labia are cut as well, and the cutter performs an infibulation, sewing up the vagina to leave one tiny opening. This is the most horrific form of FGM, which some people call pharaonic circumcision.'

Nobody said a word. The girls had stopped giggling.

I went on, explaining that the victims were never given an anaesthetic and, because of the terrible hygiene conditions in which the procedure was performed, most of them suffered infections.

For a moment I wondered whether it might not be better to spare Safa the rest of the lecture. But the girl's thirst for knowledge, her strength and her determination to help convinced me to let her stay.

'FGM is often carried out by midwives or so-called professional circumcisers,' I carried on. 'They use razor blades, shards of glass or scissors. The girls are usually cut before puberty, when they're between four and fourteen years old – though sometimes it's done shortly after birth.

'Only circumcised girls are considered pure, as you know. Most of them are married very young, because their parents desperately need the bride-price, which comes in the form of money or livestock, in order to survive.'

Safa was writing diligently on the notepad on her lap. Suddenly, she laid the pen and pad aside, stood up and turned to face her father. Frowning, she planted one hand on her hip and raised the index finger of her other hand, like a mother scolding her child. 'Papa, you mustn't do that to me,' she told Idriss, who gazed back at his daughter with a look of respect. 'You're not going to swap me for a goat . . . are you?'

Idriss caught hold of Safa's finger and bit it playfully. 'No! I'll only sell you if you don't behave,' he said – but you could hear that he was only teasing the little one. He pulled his daughter to him and tickled her stomach until she squealed.

Her childish laughter started Inab and me off too, and eased the tension that had been building in the room.

'Why do girls have this done to them?' Inab asked.

'They have all their feeling taken away to make sure that they're virgins when they get married, and that they stay faithful to their men. It basically demonstrates the power that men have over women.'

Idriss narrowed his eyes in concentration; Safa was also engrossed in what I was saying.

'FGM doesn't actually appear in the Qur'an, or in the Bible,' I went on. I explained that some people claimed it was a religious commandment. 'It is mentioned in a few surviving texts that have been attributed to the Prophet. But for one thing,' I argued, 'there's some question about whether these texts are genuine. And for another, there isn't a single passage that describes it as a duty. They say the custom is *tolerated* where it already exists. And women certainly aren't subjected to circumcision – or rather, mutilation – everywhere in the Islamic world.'

Idriss was astonished at this. He seemed like he was hearing it for the first time.

'In many Islamic countries, like Turkey,' I said, pointing

it out on a map of the world that was hanging on the wall, 'they have no tradition of circumcising women. And it's hardly ever practised in Syria, Jordan and Lebanon. But where there is a tradition of performing this cruel ritual, it's not just Muslim girls, but the children of long-established Christian families that are cut. That goes for the Copts in Egypt and the Christians in Eritrea – where the Christian and Muslim populations are about equal. The majority of Christians in Ethiopia have their daughters cut, too. There, it used to be mainly the Falashas who practised genital mutilation – and they're Jewish.'

The three looked surprised: they had always thought circumcision was a specifically Islamic ritual.

Idriss reacted more violently than expected to this information. 'What?' he cried furiously. 'That can't be right! In our mosque, the imam preaches that circumcision is God's will. He would never lie to us!'

Safa spoke up. 'The other children in Balbala told me the Devil would come and get me if I wasn't circumcised.'

Inab nodded. 'Yes, people often tell me that uncircumcised women go mad and want sex all the time. Apparently they lose control over their bodies.'

I listened, though I had already heard all the horror stories that were told to children. People invented them to justify the terrible things that were done to little girls every day.

To stop things getting heated again, I turned over the first page of the flipchart and presented my three listeners with the shocking figures I had noted there.

'According to estimates by the World Health Organisation, one hundred and fifty million women worldwide are affected by FGM. At least.' I pointed a pen at the number with all the zeros. 'Every year about three million more girls become victims of genital mutilation. That means eight thousand girls are mutilated every day.' I paused for a moment.

'Eight thousand? Every day?' Inab repeated, horrified.

'Is that a lot?' Safa asked.

'Safa, in your school there about eight hundred children. Try to imagine them all at once,' I said, to help her grasp the number.

Safa closed her eyes to picture the playground overflowing with children.

'Ten times as many girls as the children you're picturing now are going to be tortured today, tomorrow, the day after – every single day.'

The little desert flower opened her eyes wide in horror. 'That's unbelievable,' she whispered, tears welling up in her eyes.

Female genital mutilation was no easy topic for such a young child, and up until this point Safa had been very brave. But the next part wasn't meant for her ears, and we had no desire to overwhelm the girl. Juliana took Safa out for an ice-cream.

It was time to broach a particularly delicate subject: the consequences of female genital mutilation.

'During sexual intercourse, the scars from where a woman was cut usually tear open again. The pain that women feel when this happens is unimaginable. So sexuality presents a huge problem for them.'

As I had feared, Idriss suddenly looked outraged. 'What do you mean? *Ma chérie* loves me. My wife has never told me she was in pain,' he blurted out.

Inab gave him a little shove. 'Most women suffer in

silence,' she explained to him. 'Of course Fozia doesn't tell you about it. What good would it do her?'

She was absolutely right, but Safa's father dismissed her remark with a wave of his hand.

I went on: 'During childbirth, in particular, the tissue tears and there can be heavy bleeding. Women often need Caesareans, but without proper medical care, they can't be performed. Did you know that East Africa has one of the highest rates of death during childbirth anywhere in the world? And FGM is a huge factor in that.'

Idriss spoke: 'All these numbers and these terrible facts have shocked me deeply,' he began. He sounded truly shaken. 'I don't think any of this should be happening. This cruelty has to end.'

Inab opened her eyes wide in surprise. I couldn't believe my ears, either.

Then Idriss stood up and said solemnly: 'I want to join your fight. For my sisters, my countrywomen, and all the girls of this world.'

At supper that night Inab gazed despondently out of the window.

'What's wrong, Inab?' I asked, alarmed to see tears running down the girl's cheeks.

'I'm sad,' the eighteen-year-old replied, wiping her face with the back of her hand. 'I'd like to say here with you. I don't want to go back to Djibouti. It's so lovely here! I want to work with you in the office.'

Idriss and Inab both waited with bated breath for my reply. Would I allow the girl to stay, even though I had denied Idriss the same wish? He narrowed his eyes and even stopped eating for a moment. When the answer was no different to the one he had been given, his relief was palpable.

'Inab, you may be going home soon, but it's not good-bye for ever. You'll come back and visit. And if you start working for us in Djibouti, you're going to see and learn a lot. You'll also be able to put some money aside, and then you can pay your own way, and some day you'll be able to travel to any country in the world.'

Inab nodded. She knew she had a long road ahead of her.

The last few days that Idriss, Inab and Safa spent with us in Vienna went by in a flash. Juliana and I had put together a packed itinerary for the little group, and there was always something new to discover and experience.

Idriss was very impressed by Vienna's largest mosque, where Juliana took him and the two girls for Friday prayers. Safa and Inab particularly enjoyed the day-trip to a bathing hut on the Old Danube owned by a friend of Walter's, where Safa played energetically in the water.

On their last evening, I promised to visit the girls in their hotel room, to make them look beautiful for the reunion with Waris and her children.

I arrived equipped with brushes, straighteners and a make-up case, prepared to style the two girls like models.

'What's been your favourite thing about Europe so far?' I asked Safa as I tried to untangle the little one's curls.

'The big wheel was really exciting,' replied Safa, think-ing back over her stay in Vienna first of all. 'Even though we were really high up in the air, I wasn't scared at all.'

'But you nearly pooed yourself when we saw those two big dogs on the Old Danube,' the eighteen-year-old laughed at her young friend.

'Just a minute, Inab: I remember you hiding behind me when you saw those dogs,' I said in Safa's defence.

'And I'll never forget the dog in the zoo,' said the little desert flower.

'What dog?' I asked, confused.

'You know, the one that was a bear,' the girl replied, jogging my memory.

I laughed as I remembered the day in the Jardin d'Acclimatation, the huge amusement park in Paris that boasted a zoo as well as the typical fairground attractions. At the bear enclosure, a precocious little French girl of maybe four years old had explained to Safa that the dog she was admiring was actually a brown bear, which was different from koala bears and polar bears and pandas.

Safa giggled. 'And people gave you such funny looks when you pulled the goat by the horns,' she said to Inab, 'as if they were scared of goats. But they're just normal pets.'

'Oh yes!' cried Inab. 'And we went in the maze with the scary dolls. *That* was when you were really frightened, remember, Safa?'

The little desert flower nodded eagerly. 'Yes, I was really scared of the monsters. But I still went into the dark room with Sophie. That was great!' She chattered away cheerfully, recounting every step through the mirror maze and the chamber of horrors at the end. She was clearly proud of having overcome her fear.

I was astonished at the girl's memory, especially when my guests had so many new experiences to process from their time in Europe.

'You see, Safa,' I said. 'If you really want to do something, a brave girl like you can do anything at all.'

'And what did *you* enjoy most, Inab?' I said, turning to the older girl.

'When you showed us the moon through the telescope on the mountain,' she said with a smile.

'You mean the Kahlenberg,' I said, pulling hard at a lock of Safa's hair.

'Ow!' the girl squealed.

'I'm really sorry, but I have to untangle your curls before we can use the straighteners.'

Two days previously, Inab and Safa had watched me straightening my hair. 'We want to do that too!' they had cried.

I showed Inab how to use the hot iron to conjure long, smooth strands out of Safa's frizzy hair. Although I had warned Safa not to move, the little girl kept flinching, until she eventually burned her ear. 'Ow, that hurts!' she screamed, and sucked air through her gritted teeth.

'You have to suffer for beauty – that's a German proverb,' I joked. 'So be brave, we're nearly done.'

An hour later, when Safa looked at herself in the mirror, she understood the saying. 'Beauty has to suffer,' Safa repeated in her childish way.

And she was beautiful. Her dark hair looked longer, and gleamed as if she had just come from the hairdresser's. Her eyes were shining with happiness and anticipation at the thought of the journey she would make the following day.

I kissed the little one on the cheek and said: 'No, that proverb I taught you is nonsense. You shouldn't have to suffer for beauty. You shouldn't have to suffer for anything in the world, Safa!'

*

When Walter and I arrived at the hotel the following morning, all the bags and suitcases were packed and standing in a corner of the lobby, and Idriss, Inab and Safa were ready to set off. In his new jeans and T-shirt from France, with hair that had obviously been washed, Idriss looked smarter than he had ever done before. Inab had wrapped herself in a shawl, and with her bright yellow trousers and pretty white shirt on, she was literally shining. I had brought over a shimmering gold eyeshadow and some mascara for her the previous evening, and Inab had applied them both, emphasising her lovely eyes. She smiled proudly at me.

'I've got some gold on my eyes too,' said Safa, who was eager for attention as well.

In her white ruffled dress and the sandals that went with it, Safa looked as if she'd just stepped out of a children's fashion catalogue. Her carefully straightened locks were held back with the hairband from Paris. I could see that the girl's eyelids really were glittering – but realised I liked the gleam *in* Safa's eyes much better.

'It's great that everyone's ready on time,' said Walter, who had been made to wait for the chaotic group often enough over the past few days. 'Let's get going then. Maybe we'll even be in Bavaria before Waris.'

# 18

# The reunion

## Waris

A few days before, Walter had booked a holiday house in Oberammergau, a village in Bavaria that was around forty-five miles from Munich. We had the place for a week.

Mo, Hawo and Leon would also enjoy the idyllic mountain village. I could hardly wait for my son and adoptive children to meet Inab and Safa; I had told them so much about our visitors over the last few weeks. And the anticipation of seeing my beloved Safa again was really making my heart beat faster – and helping me forget my fear of a confrontation with her father.

I had arrived in the beautiful holiday house while the entourage was still on the road, and was getting impatient. I learned later that Safa had been just as impatient. 'How much further is it?' she kept asking during the six-hour drive to Oberammergau. Even when Walter stopped at a service station, she complained: 'I don't have to go to the toilet! Let's just keep driving, so we can see Waris sooner.'

It was glorious there. The clear mountain air made the summer heat bearable. The lush green of the meadows, the dreamy mountain landscape and the painted murals on the houses of Oberammergau won me over instantly. Leon, Mo and Hawo ran into the woods next to the chalet to play hide-and-seek – so I was able to enjoy the final moments of peace and quiet before our guests arrived. With a sigh, I sat down on the grass, stretched contentedly and closed my eyes.

*Toot toot toooot!* The blare of a car horn made me sit up with a start. I had fallen asleep in the sun, and hadn't noticed the car coming along the gravel road that led up the hill. I leapt up and ran to the driveway in front of the house.

'Waris, Waris, Waris!' I could hear Safa's excited voice coming from inside the car.

I pulled open the garden gate and ran to the girls. Little Safa was faster than the older Inab. She stretched her arms out as if she wanted to hug the whole world, and leapt up at me. Tears of joy welled up in my eyes.

'Safa, baby girl, my little desert flower,' I murmured, holding her tightly.

Minutes went by. I never wanted to let her go.

Then I heard Inab next to me: 'Hello, Waris,' she said in a shy, quiet voice. She sounded a little disappointed, probably because I had greeted Safa first.

I put the little one down and embraced Inab warmly as well. 'I'm so very glad to finally see you again,' I cried, taking both girls by the hand and bounding over to the car, where Walter, Sophie and Safa's father were standing. 'Hello, Idriss,' I said in a friendly voice, going up to him and extending a hand in greeting.

He stared at it uncertainly, and then unexpectedly threw his arms around me. Confused, I looked over his shoulder at Sophie and Walter, who gave me a conspiratorial wave.

Our loud voices brought the children out of the woods, and Joanna out of the house.

'Hi, I'm Hawo,' said my brother's daughter, once a grinning Joanna had also greeted the guests.

Inab and Safa looked up in fascination at the fourteen-year-old, who was already over five foot eleven. Hawo's regular, pretty features and her almond-shaped eyes put the girls under her spell at once. With her fashionable hairstyle and her casual clothes, Hawo looked like a model. In fact, she could easily have been working as one already, but I was very much against it. As proud as I was of my adoptive daughter, she had to finish school first; those modelling doors would still be open to her afterwards.

Then Mohammed, whom we affectionately called Mo, joined his younger sister. He was a good, hard-working boy as well, although life had never been easy for him. His mother had died giving birth to him and, as was the custom in Somalia, my brother had soon taken another wife, who bore him six daughters. Although Mohammed was my brother's only son, he left the boy with our mother. So Mo grew up with his grandmother in the little Somali village of Burya Khab, which means 'village of the uncircumcised'. Many decades ago, it had been home to a tribe who didn't have their daughters cut. Unfortunately, the name is no longer appropriate: there isn't a single girl in the Village of the Uncircumcised today who will be spared this horrific ritual. Which is why I was happy to have Hawo and her brother come to live with me in Poland.

'Mama's told us a lot about you already,' said Mo, who, like his sister, referred to me as his mother.

Helpful boy that he was, he took the girls' bags and led them into the house, where Leon immediately started dividing up the bedrooms.

'Mo and I are sleeping here,' he declared at once. My youngest knew exactly what he wanted. But it was impossible to be angry with the little rascal, with his cheeky face and the long eyelashes he batted innocently when he needed to. While he charged around the two-storey house, telling the guests who was sleeping where, Safa watched in fascination. She obviously liked him.

It took a while for everyone to unpack, and we finally came together as the sun went down on this exciting day. It was all very harmonious: Sophie had been shopping for food in the village, and we adults sat round the large table on the terrace, chatting and watching the children play. Even Idriss seemed relaxed. Despite what he had told me on the phone, he had so far made no move to discuss the contract with me. I was debating whether to bring the issue up myself, but I let it rest for the time being, not wanting to spoil our first evening together. I suspected that the conversation with Safa's father would be a difficult one.

'Waris, tomorrow is the big charity dinner you've been invited to,' Walter reminded me in the course of the evening. Prominent people from all over Germany were going to come together in Munich's Käfer restaurant in aid of the Desert Flower Foundation. They would also be watching some clips from *Desert Flower*. The prospect made the buoyant mood I had been in all day vanish in an instant. I stared thoughtfully into the darkness that had descended over Oberammergau.

Then I suddenly felt Safa's soft hand in mine. 'Waris, can I come with you?' the little desert flower asked.

'Of course you can, Safa,' I replied. 'The two of us will go together tomorrow evening and tell all those important people what we're fighting for.'

I stuck to my routine the following morning, and went for a run as soon as I got up. When I came back, I could hear shouts coming from inside the house. I couldn't tell who was yelling, but it was clear that something must have happened. I sprinted through the front garden, opened the door and found myself in the midst of utter chaos.

Inab, Safa and Leon were running around the house screaming, while Idriss chased after them with a large branch in his hand. I watched the four of them open-mouthed. It was only when Safa's father passed me for the third time, oblivious to my presence, that I saw what he was holding. There was a large, dark brown slug clinging to the branch, winding itself desperately around it.

Safa hid behind me, screaming hysterically: 'Help! He's got a snake and it's going to eat us up!'

'What is going on here?' I asked sternly. 'Can't I leave you alone for half an hour?'

Idriss dropped the branch in alarm, and the slug stuck itself to the floor.

'Eeeeeh!' the girls screamed, even louder than before.

'Quiet!' I shouted, putting an end to their hysterics and picking the poor creature off the floor. 'It's not a snake, it's a slug,' I explained.

The children gaped at me as I went out into the garden to put the animal on a bush. Safa followed, curious to see what I was doing. 'Safa, this slug is a living creature, just like you. I'm sure it's much, much more afraid of you than you are of it,' I explained gently.

'I'm sorry, slug,' said Safa meekly.

The rest of the day passed without further incident. I enjoyed the hours with the children that I spent in the garden, and then it was time for us to get ready for the evening.

I was just about to zip up Safa's dress when Idriss stormed angrily into the room.

'Waris, my daughter is not going to a restaurant full of strangers by herself. I can't allow it,' he spluttered.

A moment later Inab appeared behind him, wanting to go with me as well. Of course I would gladly have taken them both, but the seating was limited and we could only invite one extra person to the meal. As Safa had played an important role in the film that was going to be the centre-piece of the evening, the decision was clear-cut. But instead of listening to my explanation, Idriss and Inab just turned on their heels and left the room without another word.

'But the ceremony for the Thomas Dehler Prize is in three days,' I called after them. 'I'll take you all to that! I promise.'

There was no reply.

When we arrived at the restaurant just over four hours later, a lot of press were already waiting for us. As Safa and I got out of the car, there was a storm of camera flashes – something I was familiar with from the many red carpets I had walked in the course of my modelling career and my humanitarian work. For Safa, however, this was an entirely new experience.

When a journalist rushed up to her and asked, 'Who are you? Are you Waris Dirie's daughter?' she just looked at me in fright.

'No, this is Safa, the little girl I am sponsoring,' I answered on her behalf. 'She played me in *Desert Flower.*' At once the other photographers started trying to get a good shot of the little one as well. Safa's shyness soon vanished. She posed unselfconsciously in front of the media, explaining in French that this was her first time in Europe.

'But I'm sure I'll be back soon,' she promised. I had to laugh: once again, her self-assured, cheeky manner reminded me of myself.

Nor was she intimidated by the elegant ladies in their splendid outfits and sparkling jewellery who took their seats at our table. She chatted away cheerfully with millionaires' wives and top businesswomen, all of whom clearly liked her. After some delicious food had been served and the typical charity business was out of the way, it was time to show the clips from my film. The lights went out, and everyone looked to the front of the room in anticipation. The glow from the candles on the elegantly laid tables was the only thing illuminating the guests' faces.

A few seconds before Safa's scream echoed through the room in the circumcision scene, I reached for her hand. It was drenched in sweat. When I looked over, I could see the tension in her face, although she had been chatting happily just a little while earlier. Safa was seeing herself on screen for the first time since the film had been shot –

seeing the horrific scenes from which she had been spared in real life. *Is this too much for her?* I wondered. Or was there something else weighing on her mind at that moment?

Just then, the woman on my other side tapped me on the shoulder, looking horrified as she whispered: 'How awful!'

After the lights had come back up, Safa asked me to take her to the toilets. When we got there the little one leaned against the wall, looking exhausted. I knelt down in front of her and looked deep into her eyes.

'What's wrong, Safa?' I asked, before answering my own question: 'The scene was very hard for you, wasn't it?'

Safa stopped me with a wave of her hand. 'No, not that. But you know, Waris' – I listened intently – 'when I was watching it, I remembered something. Something I didn't want to remember.' The little one lowered her eyes.

What was she about to tell me? What had been done to her?

'Safa, talk to me,' I said, outwardly very calm, although my heart was racing so hard I could hear its wild beating.

'My grandma circumcised a lot of girls in our house,' Safa confided in a near-whisper. 'The girls screamed just like I did in the film. But I didn't really know what she was doing – until Sophie explained it to us.'

Fozia's hint had been the truth: my little Safa *was* living under the same roof as a cutter-woman. Her own grandmother earned money by mutilating girls.

'Waris,' said Safa, interrupting my thoughts. 'I'm so scared that one day they're going to circumcise me too.' She fell into my arms, sobbing.

'Sweetheart,' I whispered, 'please trust me. We have a

contract, and I'm going to talk it all through with your *papa* again. I'm sure he would *never* do anything to hurt you,' I said, without really knowing whether that was true.

Back in Oberammergau, I could see that the only light still on was in Inab's room. I whispered good-night to Walter, Sophie and Joanna. Safa, who had fallen asleep on the drive back, hung heavy on my shoulders. I crept slowly up the creaking wooden staircase to her room, where I laid her carefully on her bed. Then I went and knocked on Inab's door.

There was no sound; cautiously, I opened the door just a crack. The eighteen-year-old was lying in bed reading a magazine that Sophie had given her. She threw me a brief, sulky glance and then immediately turned away again. I went in anyway, and stood by her bed.

'Inab, you have no reason to be cross with me,' I explained to the young woman, who still wasn't deigning to look at me. 'There will be days when the two of us do something together as well. None of you should be jealous of the others. There's room enough in my heart for you all.'

Inab stared mutely at the magazine.

'I love you,' I sighed, and left the room.

Just before I shut the door behind me, I heard Inab say softly, 'I love you too, Waris.'

The next morning, Idriss too had forgotten his annoyance from the night before. He gazed with pride at the pictures of Safa and me in the local newspapers, which Walter had already been out to fetch.

'I'm famous now,' the little girl beamed.

We spent the day at a swimming pool. Safa and Leon ran riot in the large children's pool, and climbed up to the long water slide hand in hand. I was pleased to see how well the two of them were getting along. Walter, Sophie and I sat in the restaurant, going through the most important points for the Thomas Dehler Prize ceremony, which was to take place in two days' time. Safa's father had settled down on the grass by the pool with Hawo and Mo. He was contentedly puffing away on his cigarettes, and enjoying the warmth of the sun on his belly.

A loud splash made him sit up with a start. Safa had taken a run-up and had jumped into the deep pool with her usual fearlessness, sending water everywhere. I laughed out loud when I saw that Idriss had been soaked from head to foot. But he didn't find the situation quite so funny. He leapt up in a rage, pulled Safa out of the pool by her arms and smacked her on the bottom.

Before I could react, Hawo was at Idriss's side, glowering at him. 'Why are you hitting her?' she asked him angrily.

I watched her standing up for the little girl with pride in my heart.

But Idriss wasn't about to be intimidated by her. 'Safa is my daughter,' he snapped. 'The Qur'an says I can hit her if she doesn't obey me. I can hit any woman who goes against me.'

That made Hawo really angry. 'I don't think you understand. We're in Germany – in Europe. There are laws here against hitting children, women or animals.'

My adoptive daughter's already well-developed sense of justice had grown even stronger since she had moved in with me. *Good job, too*, I thought as I walked slowly over to the pool. A few of the other sunbathers had already turned to look at them, and were listening with great curiosity to Hawo and Idriss's argument. Safa's father was boiling with rage, and my adoptive daughter was also struggling to keep her cool.

Leon, Sophie and Walter rushed over to defuse the situation.

'Sister, do you want an ice-cream?' my son asked Safa, who was clearly in shock.

I went and put an arm round Hawo, who was still scowling at Idriss. 'Come on, let's go and have a coffee,' I said, walking her over to our table in the restaurant.

Sophie took Idriss to one side as well, put a can of Coke in his hand and sat down on the grass with him. He opened it without saying anything, took a sip and lit a cigarette.

'Would you like to talk to me?' Sophie asked him gently. She suspected he was feeling terribly homesick.

But Idriss didn't take her up on her offer. 'No. Nobody understands me here anyway,' he growled, and stormed off.

# 19

# The *Desert Flower* party

Our holiday together was not exactly peaceful, even if the argument at the pool had quickly simmered down again. Our different cultures and world-views were constantly clashing with each other. I realised I had to act if I didn't want the rift between my family and Safa's to become even wider: certain things needed to be aired.

I decided to organise a very special family evening.

'Today, the whole day belongs to my family,' I announced over breakfast the following morning.

Inab, Idriss and Safa stared at me with disappointment in their eyes. They obviously weren't sure if I was counting them as family too. 'Don't worry, I mean all of you,' I assured them. 'Tomorrow we're all going to the Thomas Dehler Prize ceremony together, and after that our little group will go our separate ways.' I looked around the table before going on. 'Hawo and Mohammed will fly back to Poland, to go back to school. Joanna, Sophie and Walter

**Waris, Safa and Leon.**

are going to Vienna. And Idriss, Inab and Safa' – at my words, the little girl looked down at her plate sadly – 'will go back home to Djibouti.'

Inab was the first to speak up. 'Why aren't you coming with us, Waris?'

I explained to her that this wasn't possible, because Leon and I were flying to New York to visit my oldest son, Aleeke. 'But before we have to say goodbye, I would like to have a big going-away party with you all,' I announced.

Safa's sadness vanished. 'Yes, a party: great idea!' she cried enthusiastically.

'I would like to invite you to a barbecue this evening, here in this beautiful garden,' I said. 'And afterwards we can all sit down together and watch my film.'

An awkward silence descended over the table.

'Without the film I would never have met you, Safa and Inab.' I looked gratefully at the two girls. 'It's high time we had a party for the desert flowers.'

After breakfast we all set off together to go shopping for the evening in the local supermarket. The children rushed off immediately in all directions, putting crisps, chocolate, Coke and ice-cream into the trolley. Idriss suggested buying a goat to mark the occasion, which he would slaughter personally, and then spit-roast.

'I'm afraid Oberammergau isn't Balbala,' I replied, smiling to myself. Safa's father was always making me laugh with his crazy African ways; if I was honest, these thoughts were still slumbering somewhere inside me as well. 'You can't just buy a live goat here and cut its throat. Look, that's the meat section over there. Let's go and find the best pieces.'

Idriss strode up to the counter and asked the assistant in French for goat meat. The woman didn't understand, and just looked at him blankly. Sophie hurried over to translate.

'*Goat?* We don't have that,' the Bavarian woman replied in a shrill voice.

'Then we'll take camel,' said Idriss, without glancing at his interpreter as she repeated his order word for word in German.

The Bavarian woman behind the meat counter shook her head incredulously. 'If you want camel, you'll have to drive to Munich and go to the Tierpark,' she said drily.

Idriss agreed: 'OK then, let's go the Tierpark.' I was following the discussion with amusement. 'The feet and the offal are best; they'll make a delicious stew.'

Sophie had to chuckle as well. 'Idriss, the Tierpark is a zoo, like the ones we went to in Paris and Vienna. The animals aren't sold for meat; they're just for looking at.'

Disappointed, Safa's father pursed his lips. 'OK then: antelope, please. It's expensive, but then, this *is* our going-away party.'

The Bavarian woman threw up her hands. 'No, we don't have that either! We've just got chicken, beef, lamb and pork.'

'*Pork?*' Idriss asked, as incredulous as the shop assistant had been moments before when he had ordered goat. 'You can't eat that!'

Sophie explained to the supermarket assistant that Idriss and Safa were Muslim and therefore couldn't eat pork. 'A nice bit of roast pork's still best though,' the woman muttered.

Once we had finally decided on lamb, chicken and fish, we had everything we needed for our party. With the car fully loaded, we drove back to our idyllic holiday house and began the preparations. Everyone helped: the children peeled potatoes and washed the vegetables while the adults took care of the meat. Sophie and I conjured up a delicious marinade out of olive oil, rosemary, thyme, garlic, chilli, salt and pepper.

Safa and Leon, meanwhile, had other things on their minds. They came into the kitchen hand in hand and planted themselves in front of us. My son announced solemnly: 'Mummy, I have to tell you something important. When we grow up, Safa and I are going to get married.'

Laughing, I clapped my hands together over my head. 'Leon, you're only four years old, and Safa's only seven,' I told my baby. 'You still have all the time in the world.'

Leon frowned at me, his bottom lip quivering with emotion.

Safa, who was standing silently beside him, rolled her eyes and snorted: 'Ask me again in ten years' time – you're four years younger than me anyway.'

Leon glared at his future bride. 'What?' he cried. 'Ten years? I can't wait that long!'

Meanwhile, Idriss had gathered a huge bundle of dry branches from the nearby woods and was piling them up on the ornamental lawn.

'What are you doing?' asked Walter as he came out of the house to light the barbecue.

'It's to make a big fire, so we can roast our meat,' the African explained proudly.

His face fell when Walter explained that we couldn't do that in the garden, and he started to dismantle his painstakingly constructed tower.

We were like a family in a Hollywood movie: joyful laughter rang out from every corner of the house; everyone was helping; everyone was having fun. *If only we could stop time,* I thought wistfully, gazing out of the kitchen window.

A short while later, fragrant smoke was billowing through the garden. The men had put the juicy meat on the barbecue, the table was laid and the sauces and salads were set out. To pass the time until the food was ready, the children played a last game of Mikado, while I watched them with interest. I liked this game: it revealed a lot about the character of each player. Safa was very skilful. With a steady hand and full concentration, she lifted a single stick from the pile without touching the others. Her hunger for victory glinted in her eyes. She was a winner. And when she lost, amid the cheers of the others, she started arguing and gesticulating wildly. 'No, it didn't move. You're lying!' She wasn't a good loser, but she was persistent. She had the courage to contradict the others, and defend herself. She was brave and uncompromising in a way few African girls are. At that moment I knew that one day she would be able to continue my fight. Safa *was* the little desert flower, no doubt about it.

Walter was standing by the barbecue with Idriss. 'The meat's ready,' he said, interrupting my thoughts.

When Inab and Safa came rushing up with their plates, Idriss told them off. 'Just a minute – men first.'

Hawo, who had already argued with him the previous day, didn't like that at all. 'Oh no – ladies first,' my adoptive daughter contradicted him, pushing her brother aside.

Idriss simply ignored her, taking a piece of meat off the grill and putting it on Mohammed's plate.

I couldn't stand by and watch any longer: I took the plate away from Mo and gave it to Hawo. 'Listen, Idriss,' I said sternly to Safa's father as the mood threatened to boil over again. 'In my house nobody is disadvantaged, particularly not women. We all eat together, and everyone gets the same amount.' I emphasised once again: 'I'm serious, Idriss. You come from the Stone Age, but in my house we live in modern times. Enough with these silly customs!'

His disbelief and reluctance were only too evident, but from then on Idriss handed out meat to men and women in turn. Then he helped himself to a big piece and sat down on the grass a little way off, to sulk and eat on his own.

None of us took any notice, as we concentrated on enjoying the evening. Then we went inside to begin the second part of the celebration.

You could have heard a pin drop in the living room of the timber chalet when Mo turned off the lights and started the DVD. Everyone was mesmerised by the flat screen as the vast expanse of the desert appeared in front of them. Safa sat on my lap, holding my hand very tightly. She had seen the circumcision scene already, but she seemed apprehensive about hearing her own screams again. Just as the scene began, her father leapt up and went out on to the terrace.

'Idriss,' I called, 'where are you going? Don't leave *now!*'

But he ignored me, shutting the door behind him. I couldn't believe it! I lifted Safa roughly from my lap, sat her on the sofa and stormed after him. I found him in the little pergola at the end of the garden, sitting on a wooden bench and lighting a cigarette with trembling hands.

'What's wrong?' I asked, breathless with anger at his behaviour.

He stared fixedly at his cigarette without saying a word.

'Hey, brother, tell me what's up!'

Idriss rested his elbows on the table. He balanced his right hand, with the cigarette held between his index and middle fingers, on his left fist, and pulled the smoke deep into his lungs. He exhaled long and hard. In the half-light I could his eyes were filled with tears.

'What do you think it's like for me, as a father, to see my own daughter like that?' he said, breaking the silence. 'Do you think I don't know how bad this cutting is for the girls?'

I waited a few moments before asking: 'If you know, then why don't you do something to stop it?'

'What am I supposed to do in Balbala?' he asked me, a

hard edge to his voice. 'Everyone believes it has to be done. The people are so gullible and stupid!'

Idriss looked at me accusingly before going on.

'You don't live there. You don't have to deal with it every day: the scorn, the sneering and the exclusion, the ill-will from your neighbours and the pressure from your family. We've been mocked every day since we signed that stupid contract with your foundation.'

'"Stupid contract"?' I repeated in disbelief, and raised my voice: 'That stupid contract has given you a better life! You have enough to eat, and you even have electricity in your house. Safa is going to school, and you can buy medicine for your sick son. Don't you get that?' I wasn't going to mince my words any more.

Idriss took another deep drag and gave a cynical laugh. 'Yes . . . but at what price? You have no idea how often we curse the day we signed the contract with your film people. Do you think we realised at the time what it would mean for us? You made your film, and then you went off back to Europe. But I have to live with other people's envy and resentment every day!'

His harsh words hit me like an arrow to the heart. This was just what I had been afraid of: we were being accused of abandoning people in Africa.

'Can I come and sit with you?' I asked cautiously.

He wiped the tears from his eyes with his forearm and slid along the bench.

'You have made the right decision,' I assured him quietly. 'I understand your anger and your concerns. But I promise we will always support you. Always, Idriss.'

He turned his head to me and replied with an air of resignation: 'Waris, what do you know? We are poor people.

My parents were poor, my grandparents were poor and my children will be poor. My sons have no chance; they'll never get out of Balbala. That's our fate: nobody can do anything about it. Nothing will ever change for us. There's no hope.'

For a moment I was struck dumb. There was so much misery in his voice. Safa's father had stopped believing in a better future, a better life for him and his family. I didn't know what to say.

Then a beetle fell from the tree we were sitting under and landed on the table, where it lay helplessly on its back. Idriss put out his right hand, but just as he was about to squash it I took hold of his arm and stopped him, shielding the little beetle with my other hand.

'We don't kill living things in need. We help them,' I said, taking a twig and holding it over the insect, which clung to it immediately, pulling itself up with its thin legs.

Idriss watched in surprise as the insect began to quiver, then spread its wings and buzzed off into the darkness. He laughed. 'You really do help everyone – that was just a bug.' He shook his head.

'Don't you understand, Idriss?' I replied. 'If we don't respect life, it upsets the whole structure. Even this beetle doesn't want to die. No living thing wants to die or to be unhappy. It's that simple. And that's exactly what I'm fighting for.'

Idriss held his breath.

In a quiet voice, I went on: 'So I'm fighting against the horrific genital mutilation of innocent little girls. Millions of children are being senselessly injured and killed. What for? Can you tell me?

'And I would like to help you make a better life for yourself.'

Idriss looked at me without saying anything for a moment, before standing up. He walked around the table and looked up at the clear sky, where a million stars were twinkling. Then he turned to me and said:

'I have to take my fate and the fate of my family into my own hands.'

I got up, went over and hugged him, and together we walked back to the others.

'But there are a zillion families in Balbala . . . how can we help them all?' Idriss asked me as we were about to go in through the patio door.

'We'll find a way, believe me. Your daughter is going to be a role model for girls who are under threat of FGM . . . in Balbala; in Africa; all over the world.'

# 20

# Safa is saved

A thick morning mist lay over the holiday home in Oberammergau. Everyone was still asleep, exhausted from the party. But I was feeling inspired.

I leapt out of bed, slipped into my running gear and trainers, and went out. The conversation with Idriss had unleashed energy I hadn't known I possessed. It gave me the strength for a long morning run – and for a new project that I wanted to speak to my family about straight after breakfast. And by that I meant the whole desert flower family, which included my children, my colleagues and all my foundation's supporters.

When I got back from my run, Walter, Sophie and Joanna were already sitting on the terrace, making the final arrangements for the prize-giving that evening in Munich.

'Good morning!' I called out to the group, who could see how energised I was feeling. I sat down, took a sip of orange juice and told them about my productive conversation with Safa's father.

'Idriss went so far as to say that he would like to support our work in Djibouti,' I explained cheerfully. 'All the same, you know as well as I do,' I went on in a more serious tone, 'that guaranteeing financial support is the only way to motivate other families in Balbala, and everywhere else in Africa, not to have their daughters mutilated. To protect these girls from FGM, we have to do for their families what we've done for Safa's,' I explained.

As with every new suggestion, I asked Walter, Joanna and Sophie for their honest opinion.

My closest confidante looked at me thoughtfully. 'I can imagine other families would sign a contract like that,' she said finally. 'But if we're going to give these people financial support, we'll have to carry out strict checks to make sure the girls really do stay uncircumcised. That means we need more paediatricians and midwives to work with us and give the girls regular examinations, like Dr Acina does with Safa.' Joanna was right.

'And we'll need a reliable partner in Djibouti who we can trust to pay out the money,' Sophie put in. 'We don't want the Desert Flower Foundation to lose its good reputation.'

Walter spoke up. 'There's a mother-and-child passport that exists in Europe. We should introduce something like that in Africa. Every mother who says they're prepared not to have their daughter cut will get a mother-and-child document when they sign the contract. It will have photos of the mother and daughter, with their names and dates of birth. And every three months, when the money is paid out to the mothers, it will be noted in the passport – as will each medical examination to certify that the girl is still intact.'

I loved the idea at once. 'Perfect! And if a family can't prove that their daughter is uncircumcised, they won't get the money,' I summarised.

'And there should be compulsory education for the mothers as well,' Sophie added. During her session with Inab, Safa and Idriss in Vienna, she had learned at first hand that people in Africa knew almost nothing about FGM, its fatal consequences and the senselessness of the cruel ritual.

'The women there simply don't know that they and their children have rights too,' said Joanna, agreeing with her colleague. She took a clean sheet of paper and started making notes on our conversation.

I listened attentively, relishing the collaboration with this motivated and dedicated team.

Walter wanted to formalise things straight away. 'OK then, let's write a draft. It's a plan that could certainly work. There are a lot of organisations that offer this kind of sponsorship already, but none of them actually protects girls from the crime of genital mutilation in a way that can be monitored,' he said, thinking aloud.

Safa's father suddenly appeared on the terrace, looking at us with curiosity.

'Good morning, Idriss,' I said. 'Sit down with us. We're just talking about our newest Desert Flower Foundation project.'

I gave him a quick run-down of what we were planning, and Safa's father laughed proudly. He was part of the big Desert Flower family now as well.

We carried on discussing how our new project could be

implemented and financed, having switched to French so that our guest could follow the conversation.

After a while, Idriss spoke up: 'On average, people in Balbala live on the equivalent of about thirty euros a month. A family can just about survive on that. But there's no money left over for medicine, doctors, school, clothes or a proper roof over their heads. If people in Djibouti are given a chance to earn a little more with a mother-and-child passport, they will take it gratefully and accept all the conditions. They won't have their daughters cut, because they'll have too much to lose. In any case, the bride-price they get for a circumcised girl is worth no more than a hundred euros. And that's a one-off payment. But the financial support from the Desert Flower Foundation will last several years, and the total sum paid out will be far more.'

Idriss had grasped the aim of our new idea immediately, and was now holding forth on the subject himself! There was no sign now of the dejected man who had spoken of a life of poverty and hopelessness the evening before.

'Even the most stubborn people would rather take the money for a better life than have their daughters circumcised,' he went on enthusiastically. 'Within a generation, this practice will start to be forgotten. I'm sure of it.'

Inab and Safa had come out into the garden as well, and were listening to his speech. They clapped enthusiastically. Idriss's eyes started to shine in the morning sun.

I was infected by his enthusiasm, and the prize-giving ceremony that evening was unlike any of the others I had been fortunate enough to experience. Following the events of the last few days and the constructive conversation in the morning, I was simmering with excitement at the thought of the gala that had been organised by the Thomas Dehler Stiftung in the Munich City Hall. But it was also my last evening with my friends from Djibouti, and my euphoria was tinged with sadness at the parting that was to come.

Still, I was delighted to finally be sitting beside Safa in the front row of the elegant ceremonial hall. Inab had come with us, as had Idriss, who had even borrowed a tie from my manager in honour of the occasion. Sophie, Joanna and Walter had taken their seats on his other side.

Several hundred guests had come to witness this recognition of our work. There was a video montage about the Desert Flower Foundation, after which the Federal Justice Minister, Sabine Leutheusser-Schnarrenberger, took to the stage and gave a generous laudatory speech.

'Ladies and gentlemen,' she said finally, as Safa squeezed my hand, 'I am delighted to introduce the winner of the 2013 Thomas Dehler Prize. Please welcome Waris Dirie.'

Joanna had prepared a script for my acceptance speech, but as I got up to walk to the stage I made a spur-of-the-moment decision to give it back to her. I didn't want to read from a script. This evening, I wanted to let my heart speak.

I stepped on to the stage amid thunderous applause. My wistful gaze fell on the front row, where Safa, Inab and Idriss were beaming with joy. I had grown so very fond of all three of them in the last six months. What a lot we had been through. What grave concerns we had had about little Safa. How often I had come close to despair in the battle I had fought with her father. But all the tests of our strength and our efforts to work with these people –

who had never before left their homeland – had been worth it.

I took a deep breath, brought my lips close to the microphone and began to speak.

'When I close my eyes and travel back through the years to my childhood – when I look back over my life – then I am especially proud to be able to stand here today. The girl from the desert never would have believed she'd manage to reach so many people. I'm not saying I deserve all the good things that have happened in my life. But this prize, this gesture today, is particularly important to me. I need moments like this. I need your appreciation and your recognition. They give me the strength and the motivation I need to carry on my work, and not to give up. You know, everyone is searching for happiness. But real happiness means doing the right thing. Without questioning it, without hesitating, and without wanting anything in return. That's the simplest way to experience real happiness. And believe me, it feels very good. The smile of a person I have helped is the greatest gift anyone can give me. And I think everyone should be thinking and doing these things.

'But I also remember all the lonely days when I woke up crying and filled with frustration. I often felt despair and confusion, and I kept asking myself: *Why are these terrible things happening?* But I decided to do something. Twelve years ago, my best friends and I started the Desert Flower Foundation. It would have been all too easy to go off to a desert island and put my feet up, but I wouldn't have been able to enjoy it. My heart wouldn't have been there; it would have remained with all the little girls who are made to suffer day after day.'

I let out a deep breath and looked out over the audience. They were all sitting and listening with close attention.

'You know, I have never done my work to get rich and buy a mansion, or to be famous. No, I do it so that one day I will see all girls and women – all people – happy. We people need to respect and love each other. It doesn't cost a cent. I would like to give my heartfelt thanks: I have received many other awards, and guess where most of them came from? I'll tell you: they came from Germany. So I want to get something off my chest this evening: I love you, Germany!'

The crowd cheered, and after a short pause I went on speaking.

'Everything I have done in my life I did for a single reason, with one goal in mind: to put an end to this disgusting, cruel, inhuman crime against innocent little girls. To wipe out the terrible practice of FGM once and for all.'

The audience showed their approval once again, and from the back rows I heard cries of 'It's time to put an end to it!', 'This can't be tolerated any longer!'

'This is the reason I've made a film, taken part in a lot of discussions, travelled a long way, speaking to thousands of people all over the world, and written several books. But even so, this horror is not disappearing quickly enough. I have realised that solving this problem is not just my mission; it's a mission for all of us. However, somebody had to start the fight, and that somebody was me. Not just because I was a victim of this crime myself, but because I got the sense that nobody else was going to do anything about it. Some people knew this horrific practice existed, but they just looked the other way, and hardly anybody actually did anything. I knew it couldn't go on like that. I am a mother myself, and when I hear that people are doing such awful things to their children, I can hardly believe it. And this is not just about FGM. ... No crime against children, wherever it happens in the world, should be tolerated! That is the worst thing a person can do – an adult, a father or a mother. They are supposed to protect their children, not rob them of their most valuable thing: their trust, their innocence, their childhood.'

I paused for a moment to collect my thoughts, before raising my voice again.

'I could stand here all night talking to you, but I'm going to stop there. I've got a short film to show you about a little girl: my little desert flower, Safa. I don't know how many of you have seen the film *Desert Flower*. Safa plays me as a five-year-old, when I was mutilated. I've tried so many things to open people's eyes – but often they have had no effect. So from now on, I want to try doing it another way.

'The scene you're about to see is horrific and upsetting, but it is the naked truth. Before I show the film, I want to make another big announcement. It is my new mission to save a thousand children like little Safa every year. A thousand girls a year! Will it be difficult? Yes. Will it be stressful? Yes. Will it be a hard struggle? Yes, I'm sure of that.

'Is it possible?' I turned to the audience.

'Yes!' rang out from every corner of the hall.

'Yes!' I shouted with them. 'And I'm going to do it. No: *with your help*, I'm going to do it! I want to thank you for your help, your support, your love. Thank you. It means so much to me – I couldn't do it alone. You're going to see the clip now, but first. . . Safa! Do you want to come up on stage with me, baby?'

Safa got up from the front row and walked on to the stage in her white dress. A moment later the seven-year-old from Balbala was standing before the huge audience.

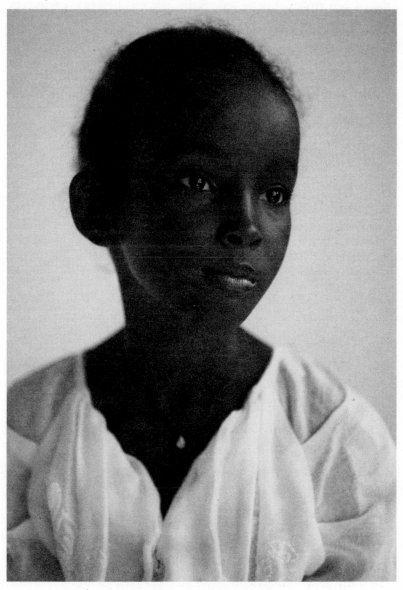

Safa's first professional photoshoot in Europe.

'This is Safa, our little desert flower, the first of a thousand girls.'

There was thunderous applause; everyone in the hall got up from their seats and clapped enthusiastically. But I didn't see them. I only saw Safa, who fell happily into my arms. I picked her up and gave her a kiss.

'Waris, I have a present for you too,' she whispered to me in front of everyone.

I peered into her little hand, where something gold was sparkling. It was the protective hand of Fatima.

# Appendix

# The Desert Flower Foundation

My friends Walter, Joanna and I founded the Desert Flower Foundation in Vienna in 2002. It was, and still is, our aim to open people's eyes and educate them about what female genital mutilation really is: a crime against innocent little girls. And we wanted things to change.

At least 150 million women are affected worldwide, and according to UNICEF, in Africa alone thirty million girls are under immediate threat of FGM.

We now know that female genital mutilation is practised not only in Africa, but also in some Asian countries. In Indonesia and Malaysia, for example, the rate of mutilation is almost 100 percent. Countless Kurdish women and girls are also affected by this terrible practice.

Following the extensive research for my 2005 book *Desert Children*, we know that many immigrants from countries where this crime is practised continue to perform FGM in their new homelands.

In 2005, over 500,000 women and girls in Europe were

affected, with another 300,000 in the USA and Canada. And there is an increasing number of cases in South America, Australia and New Zealand. Unfortunately, politicians across the world seem to have little interest in putting serious, tough measures in place to end FGM.

This gruesome practice has no place in twenty-first-century society. But without our work, the issue would quickly be swept under the carpet – and so we carry on, tirelessly confronting people all over the world, in order to help as many victims and protect as many innocent girls as we can.

Thanks to our persistence, laws against FGM now exist in almost all countries of the world, and the international media carry regular reports on the issue.

Since the Desert Flower Foundation was founded, our

Singer Joss Stone and Walter Lutschinger (far left) visit Safa and her family in Djibouti to shoot a video about the work of the Desert Flower Foundation.

efforts have led to more than 4,000 reports on FGM. The fact that so many people are interested in this issue shows me that people are taking an active interest, and they want things to change.

Since 2002, we have received and responded to more than 130,000 emails from all over the world. Every year we have over a million visitors to our website, and we reach millions more people annually through social media platforms like Facebook, Twitter, YouTube and the Desert Flower blog.

One of the mainstays of our work is to make sure that FGM remains at the forefront of people's minds, and that the situation improves for the women affected – but that is not nearly enough. I want us to achieve our goal – to put an end to this crime once and for all – as quickly as possible. And so we have started up some very promising new projects, taking a sustainable, multi-level approach to our campaign, and continuing to fight to achieve our goal.

# The Desert Flower Centre

It was a great moment for the foundation when we held the grand opening of our first centre, in Berlin on 11 September 2013. The Desert Flower Centre is a joint project by the Desert Flower Foundation and Berlin's Waldfriede Hospital.

It is the first centre worldwide where victims of FGM can receive holistic treatment and support. Alongside reconstructive surgery, it offers medical services like gynaecology, midwifery, urology, and surgery on the bowel and pelvic floor.

The Desert Flower Centre also offers psychological treatment and social care, from trained psychologists and social workers, to affected women and their families.

Dr Pierre Foldès from Paris, who has developed his own surgical technique for reconstructing the clitoris and has carried out over 5,000 successful operations on women, is on hand to advise the centre in Berlin.

Together with Dr Roland Scherer, the medical lead for the Desert Flower Foundation and head of the Berlin centre, Dr Foldès operated successfully on the centre's first two patients the day after the grand opening. Recently, Dr Scherer has been listed (not for the first time) among the 100 best doctors in Germany.

At its Berlin centre, the Desert Flower Foundation also organises workshops and seminars for girls and women affected by or under threat of FGM, along with their families. It offers training for social workers, aid workers, medical staff, teachers and employees of NGOs.

There is also a programme of cultural events, such as concerts, exhibitions, readings and film screenings, and of course charity events in aid of the Desert Flower Foundation.

The foundation has already held its first workshop for the staff of the Waldfriede Hospital.

The international media attention the centre has received has exceeded all our expectations. Other centres are now being set up in Switzerland, Turkey, France, the Netherlands, Egypt, Kenya, Ethiopia and Djibouti.

The reconstructive surgery and medical care are provided for free, financed by donations. You can find out more about the activities of individual Desert Flower centres on our website, on Facebook, Twitter and the Desert Flower blog (https://warisdirie.wordpress.com/).

# Save a little desert flower

It is my dream to save a thousand little desert flowers from female genital mutilation every year. And you can help me. You can sponsor a little desert flower yourself – and there's very little administration involved.

With a monthly donation of just thirty euros (just over twenty pounds), you can save a little girl from the certainty of being mutilated.

The foundation also uses the money to educate the girls' mothers and families, so that we can bring an end to this terrible practice. In order to collect their payment, the mothers have to take their daughters to one of the Desert Flower centres in their area. After an initial consultation, they have to sign a mother-daughter-protection contract. They pledge not to have their daughters mutilated, and to take part in a monthly FGM education workshop run by the Desert Flower Foundation where they live. They also pledge to let a foundation paediatrician examine their daughters four times a year as part of a general health check, to make sure they are still intact. They receive a mother-daughter-protection photo-ID document, where the monthly payments to the families, their participation in workshops and their daughters' health checks are recorded. The families receive financial support until the girls are fifteen.

The Desert Flower Foundation places particular value on making sure that all girls of school age are actually attending school – and when they leave, the foundation will also help them look for work.

This means that the Desert Flower centres also serve as jobcentres: I am convinced that education and economic independence are the only ways to free the women of Africa from oppression, to protect them from violence, and end female genital mutilation once and for all.

You will find further information on our website: www.desertflowerfoundation.org

If you have any questions, please email: patenschaften@desertflowerfoundation.org

If you would like to support the Desert Flower Foundation, you can donate at:

http://www.desertflowerfoundation.org/en/donate-waris-dirie-foundation/